Reprinted from
the May 1997
themed issue
of the
THE AUSTRALIAN
JOURNAL OF
LANGUAGE AND
LITERACY
VOL. 20, NO. 2
ISSN 1038 1562

The *Changing Face* of Whole Language

JAN TURBILL
University of Wollongong
Wollongong, New South Wales
Australia

BRIAN CAMBOURNE
University of Wollongong
Wollongong, New South Wales
Australia

Guest Editors

INTERNATIONAL
**Reading
Association**
800 Barksdale Road
PO Box 8139
Newark, DE 19714-8139
USA
www.reading.org

AUSTRALIAN LITERACY
EDUCATORS' ASSOCIATION
Box 78
Carlton South
Victoria 3053
Australia

Reprinted from *The Australian Journal of Language and Literacy*, Vol. 20, May 1997.

Australian Literacy Educators' Association, Ltd.
Box 78
Carlton South
Victoria 3053
Australia

IRA inventory number 9121

Contents

The Changing Face of Whole Language

About the authors

Beth Berghoff is Assistant Professor of Language Education at Indiana University–Purdue University at Indianapolis (IUPUI). Her research involves inquiry-based, multiple-ways-of-knowing curriculum, teacher education, and assessment of literacy.

> Address: IUPUI, School of Education, 902 W. New York Street, Indianapolis, IN 46202-5155, USA.

David Bloome is Professor of Education at Peabody College of Vanderbilt University, Nashville, Tennessee. He was a Fulbright Scholar at the University of Sussex, UK, in 1992–93. His latest book, *Reading Words: A Critical Commentary on the Key Terms in the Teaching of Reading*, was co-authored with Barry Stierer.

> Address: Department of Teaching and Learning, Peabody College, Vanderbilt University, Nashville, TN 37203, USA. E-mail: bloomed@ctrvax. vanderbilt.edu

Chrystine Bouffler is currently Associate Professor in the School of Education at the University of Ballarat. She has written extensively in the area of whole language and spelling and for twenty years has been working with teachers and teacher trainees to help them understand and implement whole language as an evolving theory and practice.

> Address: School of Education, University of Ballarat, PO Box 663, Ballarat, Victoria 3353, Australia. E-mail: c.bouffler@ballarat.edu.au

Brian Cambourne is currently at the University of Wollongong and has been lately involved in developing professional development materials in literacy and assessment and evaluation of literacy.

> Address: Faculty of Education, University of Wollongong, Northfields Avenue, Wollongong, NSW 2522, Australia. E-mail: Brian_Cambourne@uow.edu.au

Mem Fox is passionate about literacy and its development. Until the end of 1996, half her life was spent teaching literacy studies with zest and enormous happiness at Flinders University. She is now a full-time writer for the first time and an occasional literacy consultant in Australia and the United States.

> Address: c/o Australian Literary Management, 2a Armstrong Street, Middle Park, Victoria 3206, Australia.

Jerome Harste is currently Professor of Language Education at Indiana University where he teaches courses in reading and writing education. He has done extensive research in the fields of early literacy, reading comprehension, and teacher education.

Address: 3036 Education Building, Indiana University, Bloomington, IN 47405, USA.

Chris Leland is currently Associate Professor of Education at Indiana University–Purdue University at Indianapolis, where she teaches courses in literacy education and works with teachers and students at the Centre for Inquiry.

Address: IUPUI School of Education, 902 W. New York Street, Indianapolis, IN, 46202-5155, USA. E-mail: cleland@iupui.edu

Jo-Anne Reid teaches English curriculum at the University of Ballarat. Her research interests focus on the pedagogical practice of teaching and learning literacy in early childhood to tertiary settings.

Address: School of Education, University of Ballarat, Ballarat, Victoria 3353, Australia. E-mail: jreid@ballarat.edu.au

John Smith has worked as an elementary school teacher in New Zealand, England, and Canada. He is currently working at Dunedin College of Education in the field of teacher education. His most recent work is (with Warwick Elley) *Learning to Read in New Zealand*.

Address: Dunedin College of Education, Union Street East, Private Bag, Dunedin, New Zealand. E-mail: Jws@dce.ac.nz

Jan Turbill lectures at the University of Wollongong. Her research ranges from early literacy development to professional development. This work underpins the staff development program, FRAMEWORKS.

Address: Faculty of Education, University of Wollongong, Northfields Avenue, Wollongong, NSW 2522, Australia. E-mail: Jan_Turbill@uow.edu.au

David Wray is Reader in Literacy at the University of Exeter and Director of the EXEL project. **Maureen Lewis** was Research Officer on this project and is now Lecturer in Education at the University of Plymouth.

Address: David Wray, School of Education, University of Exeter, Exeter, EX1 ZLU, UK. Maureen Lewis, Faculty of Education, University of Plymouth, Rolle Campus, Exmouth, Devon, UK.

Lorraine Wilson works as an educational consultant. Much of her consultancy involves her in teaching in classrooms around teachers' needs. She is presently the convertor of Teachers Applying Whole Language (TAWL), a Special Interest Group of ALEA. In 1996 Lorraine was a recipient of the ALEA Medal.

Address: 81 Amess Street, North Carlton, Victoria 3054, Australia.

Guest editors' introduction

We were excited to have the opportunity to edit this issue on whole language as we believe such a focus is both timely and necessary. Timely because of the intensity of the debate that has been taking place about the nature and efficacy of whole language (both here and overseas); and necessary because of the confusion and division that this debate is creating among teachers, parents, academics, and politicians.

It is also important from the perspective of the politics of representation, that is how things get "named." As Knoblaugh and Brannon (1993) claim, "How things are named, who gets to do the naming, what motives are involved, what consequences follow, what possibilities for alternative naming...[can be] forgotten or [go] unrecognized, or [be] ignored, or suppressed..." (pp. 3–4) is important in creating an informed citizenry.

In recent times the whole language story seems to have been hijacked and retold in the main by its adversaries. The articles in this issue serve to redress this imbalance by providing an alternate telling by some of its advocates and practitioners.

The theme of this issue, *The postmodern face of whole language*, is apt given the current educational and political climate. It provides a useful framework for the whole language advocates and practitioners who have written in this issue to tell their stories, while demonstrating that whole language philosophy and its pedagogy have an important place in the literacy education of our children in this postmodern era.

There are some who will argue that (something *they* call) whole language was a fad of the 1980s and having had its day should be relegated to the "museum of educational innovations" (Hargreaves, 1994, p. 60). The articles in this issue form a cumulative and resounding response to this claim. They demonstrate that whole language is alive and healthy, albeit a little worse for wear from the effects of uninformed and often deliberately malicious naming or labelling and a lack of understanding of the changes and change processes that whole language philosophy and its related pedagogy have experienced over the years.

1

We believe these issues are related and can be illustrated by a story that Turbill likes to share:

> I remember well one of the first questions asked of me when I began my academic career as a part-time undergraduate student was "And how would you label yourself?" A little confused by the question, I responded quietly, "A teacher."
>
> "Yes, but what sort of teacher?" retorted my tutor.
>
> "A kindergarten teacher," I responded, feeling more and more self-conscious about what seemed to me to be rather silly questions.
>
> Finally, with an exasperated tone, the tutor said, 'Yes, but what philosophy do *you* follow as a kindergarten teacher?
>
> Now I was stumped. I didn't have a label to give to what I did and believed as a kindergarten teacher. I could list the things I believed to be important in my teaching, I could list what I thought were the best ways to teach my children. I could list all the things I wanted and expected my kindergarten children to learn by the end of the year with me as their teacher. But to give all this a label or one name of any kind seemed impossible to me. I found myself going all hot and feeling very stupid as I responded, "I don't know."
>
> I had learned from this brief discussion in my first tutorial that there must be a name for what I thought and did and indeed if I was to sound academic I needed to find out what I was! By the end of my first year I had read enough in educational psychology to decide that I was a *humanist*. I felt better having a label. As the years went by, I discovered there were some other labels that seemed to fit my view of the world of education. These included *process-oriented* and *meaning-focussed* in the 1970s. Then I heard the label *whole language*, and I decided that seemed to encapsulate what I thought and did. Since then I really liked the label *holistic*, and more recently *constructivist* and *postmodern*. So after some twenty years studying my way through a B.A., M.Ed., and Ph.D., I think I can now answer the question asked of me.
>
> I am a humanist, whole language, constructivist, postmodern teacher! Do I need *all* these labels in order to be an effective teacher? No, of course I don't. There are elements of each in all these labels, and so I

will stay with the label that reflects language and literacy education and say, "I am a whole language teacher!" However, I am quick to add, "I am a humanist at heart, who has a constructivist view of knowledge and learning operating within a postmodern society!"

The main point of this short story is that we can really only label our thinking and set of beliefs after we have become aware of the labels that others use to encapsulate certain concepts and philosophies. When we understand the concepts that these labels represent, we begin to wear them to signify that we want to belong to a particular philosophical club. We don't have to do this in order to teach effectively but, being social beings, we have a need to belong. And being part of a social group that has similar beliefs and practices means we develop a shared language and a sense of community. We can challenge, share, reflect, and learn together in a supportive and trusting environment in what Barth (1990) refers to as a "community of learners." Once labelled, however, we then feel the need to support each other and defend ourselves and others when it seems that our club and its members are under attack.

On the other hand, there is the danger that some teachers will grab at a label because it is the latest fashion, or newest "club" to which to belong. This practice can be detrimental to these teachers and their students as they join the club for the wrong reasons. They do so without deep reflection or a sense of commitment to the particular set of beliefs which frame and guide the club (our present educational culture, we believe, encourages teachers to do just this). They need to become members of the latest club simply to feel that they belong somewhere. They can then get on with what they are doing without further interference. It feels safe. Sadly, such teachers are peripheral members who don't really know what is going on, and when the time comes, they will quickly give up membership of one club for another. At best, these teachers try a few different strategies in their classrooms but generally little changes. At worst, they confuse students, parents, and other teachers.

So what of the label whole language, given to a grassroots movement of literacy educators in the 1980s. The term itself seems to have appeared some ten years after the movement away from traditional skill-based literacy teaching had begun and a new philosophy had emerged. Such a paradigmatic change in language and literacy education occurred at the same time as society generally was showing "signs that the age of modernity may have been approaching its end" and a "change that we have come to call postmodernity" (Hargreaves, 1994, p. 31) was taking place.

David Elkind (1995) supports this claim when he says:

> The school is the mirror of society and of the family. As society and the family change, so too must the school. Over the past half century, there has been a major structural change in how we think about, perceive, and value ourselves and our world. This change has transformed our arts and our sciences, our industries and commerce, and our families. It has been labelled the shift from modernity to postmodernity. Of necessity the school has reflected these changes and is a far different institution today than it was at midcentury. This transformation of the school has come about not by a conscious pursuit of education reform, but rather an adaptive response to the changes in the family and in the larger society. (p. 8)

Once labelled, whole language philosophy and its pedagogy became "things" and, as such, could be either revered or attacked. During the 1980s, the whole language club was *the* club to be seen at and belong to, and many teachers quickly joined, with too many of them not really knowing or really wanting to know the basic philosophy underpinning the existence of the club. As we entered the 1990s, there were some who became dissatisfied with their membership and moved out to begin their own clubs. There were others who never joined the whole language club and remained suspicious of its philosophy and practices. These groups became the critics of whole language; some were useful allies, others were bitter and bigoted enemies.

As those of us who remained in the whole language club questioned, discussed, and reflected on issues in our small field of knowledge and discourse, others (allies) were doing similar things in their fields—pushing back, forward, to all sides. What began as a slow paradigm shift began to gain momentum as the different fields of knowledge and their discourses joined in symbiotic and synergistic relationships. Debates, critiques, and further challenges forced those of us in whole language to continue to explore, reflect, and look further afield in order to respond to these debates and challenges. In doing so, whole language has continued to develop into a more mature and sophisticated philosophy—one that reflects many fields of knowledge and discourses, having imported much from sociology, linguistics, epistemology, psychology, psycholinguistics, learning theory, and hermeneutics, among others. In other words, whole language theory grows and evolves like the human nervous system, constantly forging and forming new networks of relationships as knowledge and understanding about children, language, learning, language learning, and cultural issues continue to emerge.

Whole language, therefore, should not be viewed as a stepping stone along a chronological history of literacy knowledge, one that has been stepped over as educators move onto "critical theory." Rather, whole language should be seen as a philosophy that has been both shaped by, and is an agent of, societal changes within a postmodern era. As whole language matured, it has changed. It no longer looks the same as it did when it was a neophyte. While the basic essence or tenets have remained the same, its form, structure, and the way it is realised in practice have altered. The difficulty the whole language club faces is that outsiders have not been privy to these changes and developments and thus do not recognise the more mature philosophy.

This process of change can be likened to the growth and development of a child. When a child is born, we label that child—in this case, Sam. Sam grows and matures over the years. By the time he is four, he looks, thinks, and acts very differently from how he did four years ago or even one year ago. Yet he is still Sam. The essence that made Sam four years ago is still there deep inside him and always will be, but Sam will continue to grow and mature and change. However, he will always be labelled Sam (unless he chooses to change his label). Those who do not see him often and know him well may no longer recognise him after several years. They will remember him as he was at one or two, yet they will expect that he will mature and change. And so it should be with whole language. Those of us who know it well know that it has changed, grown, and developed in both philosophy and practices. We know that it will continue to change and grow as the thinking and practices are challenged and reflected upon by its advocates. We hope that the articles in this issue will enlighten those who have not seen the postmodern face of whole language while at the same time support and encourage those who know it well.

Jan Turbill and Brian Cambourne
Guest editors

REFERENCES

Barth, R. (1990). *Improving schools from within*. San Francisco, CA: Jossey-Bass.

Knoblaugh, C., & Brannon L. (1993). *Critical teaching and the idea of literacy*. Portsmouth, NH: Boynton Cook.

Hargreaves, A. (1994).*Changing teachers, changing times: Teachers work and culture in the postmodern age*. London: Cassell.

Elkind, D. (1995, September). School and family in the postmodern world. *Phi Delta Kappan, 77*(1), 8–14.

Whole language: Are we critical enough?

Beth Berghoff, Jerry Harste, and Chris Leland

Our colleagues from Indiana University in the United States, Berghoff, Harste, and Leland, challenge those critics who suggest that there is not a critical focus in whole language philosophy. Their thoughtful response in this article addresses those critics and leaves us with some further challenges for a postmodern era.

In the newspaper today, the headline says: "Economy demands higher standards for all students." The article, written for our local newspaper by "the nation's premiere urban and regional growth expert," decries the failure of our public schools to prepare children for the twenty-first century and suggests a simple solution:

> The Indianapolis region needs hard debate about standards—the objective math and English, computer and analytic skills—that the region's employers and citizens expect of its graduates. Regular tests, school-by-school, should be conducted across the region... (Pierce & Johnson, 1996, p. D7)

Tomorrow our jobs as whole language educators will be more difficult. Many people will have had their beliefs reinforced: Good education depends on grade-by-grade standards and rigorous testing; literacy equates to having objective English skills; process or inventive work is a waste of time. As whole language educators, we hold beliefs radically different from these educational conservatives. We don't think of school as a place where children learn only objective skills. We think of school as a place where we continually ask ourselves, our children, and their families what kind of world we want to live in and how we can create that world.

Operating on the tenets of whole language, our work is anything but simple. Our understanding of the dimensions involved in learning, in social practices, and in democracy and justice continue to grow more complex. Each year, we integrate more perspectives into the work, and each of us in the community takes responsibility for constructing our own working knowledge. This means that no two individuals practice whole language exactly the same way, although we agree on basic fundamental principles about language, learning, teaching, curriculum, and social practices.

This theoretical foundation holds that knowledge is constructed by individual learners within the social context (Whitmore & Goodman, 1996), and that education is potentially transformative (Boozer, 1996). Rather than looking at children from a deficit view, whole language educators focus on the strengths of each learner and on supporting each learner's developing voice through meaningful social interactions, writing, and literature. We value the use of students' home languages, of functional spelling, and of multiple interpretations of written texts. We create communities where it is safe for learners to be who they are, and where it is possible to explore other worlds and relationships.

Currently, we are experiencing backlash to our whole language position. The media echoes the sentiments of mainstream culture, and we find ourselves in a defensive position. Our beliefs and practices position us outside of the invisible centre of traditional assumptions about teaching and learning. Our work not only directly challenges the authority of the dominant view of education, but also the whole social framework of our culture and the ways we think about it (Ferguson, 1990). This makes us dangerous. As long as the invisible centre remains unchallenged, its power remains intact. But if that authority breaks down, there remains no point relative to which others can be defined. In other words, the dominant norms of the culture, which are seldom overtly acknowledged, are jeopardised by the whole language community because we are envisioning and creating new possible ways to work and live together. People who benefit from the system operating on the existing norms have much to fear from us. If whole language becomes the norm at some point in time, power relations will move away from domination and toward caring and valuing diversity. Our culture will be different.

We are learning what it means to be critical of the status quo, to challenge the invisible centre. When a nationally televised news journal contrasted whole language with direct instruction and made whole language look like it was hopelessly failing a generation of elementary students, we knew we were making people uncomfortable. When whole language was blamed for the low reading levels in California, we knew we were scapegoats. We have become powerful enough to merit control. And whether we like it or not, we have to think about ourselves differently. As members of the whole language community, we are people who choose to believe in principles that stand in critical opposition to the dominant ideology. Our work is political.

Given the attacks on whole language and our developing understanding of the political implications of whole language (Shannon, 1992), some have criticised whole language educators for not being critical enough in their perspective, for focussing on issues of pedagogy instead of issues of social concern. Discussions about teaching phonics in the context of reading and writing or about the best form of spelling instruction seem trivial when compared to questions about how we might help children understand the social and political forces acting on their lives. In this article, we refute the criticism that whole language has not been critical by exploring the ways that whole language has been successful in challenging some of the norms of education. We will also explore some of the ways that whole language has not been critical enough and look at how our notions of critical literacy are pushing us to consider the larger implications of our beliefs and practices.

Whole language has been critical

The whole language community has learned how to construct knowledge socially. As individuals, we thoughtfully move between theory and practice, contributing our new insights and questions to the ongoing dialogue among community members. This makes us particularly irritating. From our place on the margin, we continually develop new ideas and practices that contest the invisible centre. In this way, whole language has been critical and has interrupted the normalised text of education. For example, almost twenty years ago, whole language proponents introduced the notion that reading is a meaning-making process that depends on using the language subsystems of graphophonics, syntax, and semantics in an ongoing cycle of prediction and confirmation. In an era of skills-driven basal programs, whole language teachers began saying that reading instruction should not focus on direct instruction of phonics, vocabulary, syllabification, and other skills, but rather on meaningful reading itself. These teachers began to immerse students in written texts in much the same ways that children are immersed in oral language when they learn to speak. The teachers read aloud, read aloud, and read aloud (Fox, 1995). They brought hundreds of books into their classrooms and loads of other reading materials like comics, newspapers, and magazines. Children were given freedom of choice of reading materials, and in many classrooms trade books eventually replaced the basal anthologies, writing replaced the worksheets, and grand conversations (Peterson & Eeds, 1990) replaced the comprehension questions. What began as marginal practice has moved into the mainstream: Reading aloud to children and providing time for sustained silent reading are thought of as standard practice in any complete language arts program.

Another place where whole language has interrupted the invisible centre is related to writing, the identity of the writer, and the writing process. Whole language teachers, believing in the power of kidwatching (Goodman, 1978), collaborative community, and meaningful reasons to write, pursued the authoring cycle as a curricular structure (Harste, Short, & Burke, 1985). Instead of focussing on the surface level of language and responding to students' spelling and punctuation errors, whole language teachers responded to the meaning in a child's writing and supported each child with timely demonstrations and revision strategies. They invited children to write from their own life experiences and continued to emphasise that it was not the procedure that mattered, but the students' participation in the "literacy club" (Smith, 1988).

The whole language community's theory of language development became more sophisticated as teachers documented the writing development of children for each other. In the early grades, this shift in theory and practice opened the door to more authentic early literacy practices. Many whole language lower primary teachers now understand that their children do not have to wait until they know all the letters and sounds to write in meaningful ways. They value approximations and encourage functional spelling. In the upper primary grades, whole language teachers incorporate writing into every learning minute, taking advantage of its power as a reflective and communicative tool. Again, the work begun on the margins has come to the centre. Publishers now produce handbooks to use during the writing process in lieu of books full of discrete language skill exercises. Whole language has been critical. Looking back, we can see that whole language has challenged the invisible centre and even seeped into the centre in some cases. It has challenged and changed some fundamental beliefs and practices related to language learning in schools.

Whole language and critical literacy

The attacks mounted against whole language have forced us to clarify what makes us threatening. We know that we now have to put more effort into being articulate and clear about our theory. We also know that it is not really the changes we have brought about in reading and writing that cause the opposition to strike out at us. It is our constant redefining of literacy and our insistence that schools must serve all learners.

We did begin our journey with a focus on using whole language in classrooms. Along the way we learned that more than language is involved in literacy. As we wrote with children, we experienced some violent and painful stories of bias, discrimination, and neglect. As we read with children and put meaning at the centre of reading, we learned that reading could not be divorced from the lives of children. We learned that literacy is not just about language—it's also about social practices and our witting or unwitting roles as cultural agents. We learned that we cannot be concerned just with the culture of the classroom, but we must also look beyond to the political and social struggles outside. We must understand culture and the effects of living in a multicultural world.

As whole language educators, we are feeling a lot of tension about what we have learned. On the one hand, we recognise that whether we are conscious of it or not, our work always has social and political implications. To be true to our principles, we need to take a transformative stance. As one critical theorist puts it:

> ...if we do not teach in opposition to the existing inequality of races, classes, and sexes, then we are teaching to support it. If we don't teach critically against domination in society, then we allow dominant forces a free hand in school and out. (Shor, 1990, p. 347)

On the other hand, we do not believe that we have the right to make our will dominant over others, and that leaves us in a particularly vexing situation. How do we challenge the systems of gender, race, and socioeconomic oppression that act as barriers to equality and justice without assuming an authority we neither want nor believe anyone should have? How can we be both critical and open enough to invite people into a dialogue about these systems?

Street (1995) has helped us with this dilemma by writing about different perspectives we could assume as we begin to carve out a critical literacy stance that allows us to work within this tension. He suggests we work on an approach that would develop in children an awareness of the socially and ideologically constructed nature of language, literacy, and society. Luke (1995) also suggests that we attend to the face-to-face aspects of literacy, recognising that critical literacy is about power as a process rather than authority and domination. It entails deciding when to speak, when to be silent, or when to commit something to print. It is a matter of considering the social relations of power around texts, asking: Who is trying to do what? To whom? With and through what texts? It is a stance wherein an individual constantly examines and creates a personal identity that has the disposition to rethink how perspectives and identities are constructed, how knowledge is produced, and how dominance is maintained.

Clearly, we whole language folk are once again in uncharted waters. We have to learn how to be more critical as teachers without risking indoctrination. We want our work to help learners break through the barriers of race, gender, and social class, so we are consciously asking how our daily decisions and practices contribute to the maintenance of these systems. We are thinking collaboratively about the texts we choose to use with learners and the questions we ask about those texts. We are critical of stereotypes and power arrangements that disadvantage some of our students, paying special attention to the ways that language relegates individuals to the margins. And we are consciously attempting to educate ourselves by seeking out the stories of persons whose experiences are different from our own, so that we may know about multiple literacies and literacy practices.

We argue about whether we should be front-loading critical issues into the curriculum, deliberately introducing issues of gender and race, or whether these issues should emerge from the questions and concerns of the students. It seems that many of the issues we want to examine come up without much deliberate effort.

We know teachers who do not purposely choose books and activities that raise critical issues, but instead bring their own heightened awareness of these issues to the classroom and listen for children's questions and observations. When the children begin asking why all the boys work together all the time or why the rainforest is disappearing, teacher Vivian Vazquez (1996) encourages further exploration. She extends their thinking so that the critical implications of their questions become evident. She finds that children are quite capable of recognising where problems exist and how they might take action.

Others of us are interested in being more overt. Altwerger (1996) suggests we should let the world into our classrooms and help students to critique the problems and develop social action aimed at change. We can use literature to expose learners to multiple perspectives about the world, both past and present. For instance, Altwerger suggested the following books should be included in a text set about Thanksgiving, a holiday that celebrates the colonisation of the United States: *Going Home*, a story about a Mexican American homecoming; *Baseball Saved Us*, the story of Japanese children in an internment camp during World War II; *Who Belongs Here?*, an exploration of the diversity of people in the United States; *Fly Away Home*, the story of a homeless father and son who live in an airport; and *The Elders Are Watching*, a story representing the Native American perspective on history. A text set like this presents many opportunities to interrogate the links between our current social practices and those of our past. Learners can be introduced to the idea that they are situated within a complex system of social practices that are subject to change through social action. This awareness does not come without cost, however. It can be painful, and unless our pedagogy enables our students to have hope, it may add to the stress of living in a world where people are unempowered and oppressed.

We also look more critically at texts. We read a story like *When the Relatives Came* and enjoy it for its literary qualities and as a portrayal of Appalachian culture, but then we ask whether the portrayal is fair. Who benefits from this story? Who does not? How would the story would be different if it were told about an African American or Hispanic family? How would we tell such a story about our own family?

Is whole language critical enough?

To answer this question, each of us has to consider our own context. There is more to being critical than just speaking out against inequities. As we grow toward understanding the ways that our teaching helps to shape the world we live in, we are becoming more sensitive to the things we say and do. We cannot directly teach the ideas that are most important to us. Rather, we create the opportunities for learners to construct these ideas for themselves. As a community, we have been fairly successful in doing this with language instruction, in part because we became very knowledgeable about language and the processes of language. Perhaps the new challenge is to become equally knowledgeable about the social practices of literacy. We have to understand culture, history, our multicultural world, and the social and political forces that act on our lives. We have to learn how to dismantle faulty assumptions about societal structures in much the same way that we learned how to dismantle faulty assumptions about language.

Are we critical enough? Generally speaking, we are not activists who openly challenge decisions in the political arena, but we have a history of creating new possibilities. We have successfully moved important ideas from the margin to the centre. We did this by being avid learners and articulate teachers. We have not been critics so much as knowledge generators. In the final analysis, the one thing we know that whole language does and does well is help a learner or a community of learners interrogate their values. It is this aspect of the theory that gives us hope.

REFERENCES

Altwerger, B. (1996). *Imagining our possibilities*. Keynote address presented at 86th Annual Convention of National Council of Teachers of English: Day of Whole Language, Chicago, IL.

Boozer, M. (1996). Confronting the deficit view...again. *Talking Points*. Plymouth, MN: Whole Language Umbrella.

Ferguson, R. (1990). Introduction: Invisible centre. In R. Ferguson, M. Gever, T. Minh-ha, & C. West (Eds.), *Out there: Marginalisation and contemporary cultures*. Cambridge, MA: Massachusetts Institute of Technology Press.

Fox, M. (1995). *Putting on the brakes: Avoiding the wrecks in whole language*. Paper presented at Children's Literature Conference, Butler University, Indianapolis, IN.

Goodman, Y. (1978). Kidwatching: An alternative to testing. *National Elementary School Principal*, *57*, 41–45.

Harste, J., Short, K., & Burke, C. (1985). *Creating classrooms for authors: The reading-writing connection*. Portsmouth, NH: Heinnemann.

Luke, A. (1995). When basic skills and information processing just aren't enough: Rethinking reading in new times. *Teachers College Record*, *97*(1), 95–115

Peterson, R., & Eeds, M. (1990). *Grand conversations: Literature groups in action*. New York: Scholastic.

Pierce, N., & Johnson, C. (1996, November 17). Economy demands higher standards for all students. *Indianapolis Star*, p. D7.

Shannon, P. (1992). *Becoming political: Readings and writings in the politics of literacy education*. Portsmouth, NH: Heinemann.

Shor, I. (1990). Liberation education: An interview with Ira Shor. *Language Arts, 67*, 342–353.

Smith, F. (1988). *Joining the Literacy Club: Further essays into education*. Portsmouth, NH: Heinneman.

Street, B. (1995). *Social literacies: Critical approaches to literacy in development, ethnography and education*. White Plains, NY: Longman.

Vazquez, V. (1996, November). Paper presented at a gathering of Indiana University graduate students, Bloomington, IN.

Whitmore, K., & Goodman, K. (1996). Practising what we teach: The principles that guide us. In K. Whitmore & Y. Goodman (Eds.), *Whole language voices in teacher education*. Urbana, IL: National Council of Teachers of English.

This is literacy: Three challenges for teachers of reading and writing[1]

David Bloome

Bloome identifies three challenges facing whole language educators and others interested in education and democracy. He argues that these challenges are part of broader social and economic changes that are occurring in the United States and other countries. He believes that how whole language advocates respond to these challenges will determine what whole language ultimately becomes.

There is no single definition of literacy. What counts as literacy at a particular time and place depends on who has the power to define it. Like schools, the defining of literacy is done both by individuals and institutions. Indeed, how literacy is defined is full of conflict that goes beyond technical questions about best ways to teach it. Rather, it revolves around social, cultural, and economic issues.

Whole language educators have historically sought to decentre the authority of a monolithic and elitist view of reading and writing. Unlike totalising theories that claim universality and must remain abstract and disembodied, whole language theories (for there are many) must remain close to and defined by people's experiences with reading, writing, and language, including the experiences of teachers and students in classrooms and communities. Viewed in this manner, whole language can provide an approach to theorising and educational practice that hovers close to the realities of people's daily lives, reflecting changes in our lives and in the conditions in which we live.

---

[1]This article is a revised and shortened version of a talk the author gave at the Whole Language Umbrella Conference in Melbourne, Australia, September 1996.

This article focusses on three challenges that are facing whole language educators and others interested in education and democracy. These challenges are part of broader social and economic changes that are occurring in the United States and other countries. How whole language educators address these and other challenges will define whole language in the future and determine its value.

The first challenge is the separation of process, content, people, and emotion in how language is defined and taught. I take the position that there is no language without people using it to do real things in a real and material world. The second challenge involves the pedagogisation of reading and writing.[2] Rather than the locating of literacy in community, family, and work settings, the classroom has become the dominating setting and intellectual framework for children's and adults' literacy. The third challenge is the commodification of language. Instead of defining reading and writing as verbs, as something that people do to others with written text, reading and writing are being defined as nouns—as a things that can be broken up into pieces, which can be acquired, owned, and sold (Street & Street, 1991; Willett & Bloome, 1992).

The separation of process, content, people, and emotion in defining and teaching language

In the United States (and elsewhere), there have been several efforts at separating out and removing language from people, from a part of our daily lives. One of these means is the formulation of language as idealised, reduced to syntax and grammar, ignoring what people do with it. This includes those formulations of language that take no account of how people struggle with meaning's elusiveness or how language is used to inflict suffering or create caring. This separation of language from people's lives is part of an ongoing technologisation of knowledge, including knowledge of language. We take common words

---

[2]Both the phrase "the pedagogisation of reading and writing" and many of the ideas discussed under this rubric are borrowed from Street and Street (1991). I have also heavily borrowed from a manuscript by Willett and Bloome (1992).

filled with meaning, history, and emotion and replace them with sterile technical terms. Here are two examples. First, our discussion about the word *motivation* from *Reading Words* (Stierer & Bloome, 1995):

> In the teaching of reading, *motivation* is primarily used to express concern about students who are not motivated to read or to learn to read. Questions are typically asked about how a student can be motivated to read. And typically the answers focus on providing *motivation* (rewards for reading), appealing to the student's inherent *motivation* (providing books that appeal to the student's interests), or on improving the student's character (counselling the student to develop intrinsic *motivation* to read).
>
> The question of how to motivate a student to read emphasises the action of *motivating*, a transitive verb, doing something to someone. The answers transform the verb—*motivate*—into a noun, a quality that a student either has or doesn't have. When defined as a noun, teachers are viewed as creating *motivation* and then giving it to their students. By transforming motivate into a noun, the agency involved in *motivation* is neutralised. *Motivation* is not defined as somebody doing something to someone, but as a commodity that students can have lots of or little of. As a quantity, students can be held accountable for having or not having sufficient *motivation* to read, and teachers can be held accountable for not providing enough *motivation*.
>
> It is interesting to contrast *motivation* and desire. Desire is associated with passion, romance, love, and sex. Desire has substance. Even when desire is used metaphorically—"I hope you will have a desire to read the book"—desire nonetheless carries a sense of passion and sexual energy. We often speak of the content and characters of books as showing desire and passion.... By contrast, readers are not conceived of as having desire and passion, instead they have *motivation*. Desire and passion are kept textual and fictional. By stripping students of desire and renaming it *motivation,* the task of getting people to do something, like reading—whether it is something they want to do themselves or something others want them to do—becomes a technological task rather than a moral and political one involving the full range of human emotions, desires, and passions. (p. 54)

A second example comes from a kindergarten classroom (Bloome, 1994), where I watched a lesson on spring. The children sat on the floor and the teacher put pictures associated with spring—the sun, the wind, flowers, a kite—on the felt board. The group discussed items, such as the Easter Bunny, popularly associated with spring. The students were then directed to their tables to draw pictures of spring. I videotaped a group of boys undertaking the task. On one side of the paper they drew traditional pictures, but then they turned over their papers and, looking at each other, they began pictures like that in the figure below.

As they drew they vigorously talked with each other. Here's what the child who drew the picture said as he worked. He began by showing the more traditional looking picture he had drawn.

> *This is me flying my kite, the wind came along and blow my kite that's a little...* Then he flipped over the sheet and, referring to the drawing shown on previous page, *that's when the storm started to come, when the bad, the tree caught on fire, the wall busted down and let's see the plane caught on fire and started round in a whirlpool, the sun got sucked up like the tree and let's see, and a, water came up and made it worse, the sun got sucked up and that's about it.* (Bloome, 1994, p. 64)

Figure   Kindergarten student's drawing of spring

How shall we analyse this child's text? Discount it because he does not talk in complete sentences? Search for underlying grammatical forms and make tree diagrams? Create a semantic structure to reveal its intricate ideational and interpersonal meanings? Do we segment it into components for story grammar analysis? Do we dismiss it completely as irrelevant to the study of language because it will not answer the questions that some linguists think we should ask?

Such questions are worse than being merely technical and absurd. They rob us and those kindergarten children of language. The questions that we need to ask of language must follow our and our students' uses of it and the meanings, emotions, pain, joy, and caring it has in our and their lives.

The pedagogisation of reading and writing

Once a ninth grade student in my remedial reading class failed a test on "Understanding Character." The remedial reading program that I was directed to run involved a series of competencies, failure at one preventing forward movement on others (Bloome, 1983). The test involved a short passage about a cranky student who gave the teacher a hard time, and I asked my student to explain his answers, hoping to gain insight into why he had failed. One multiple-choice question was as follows:

Faced with the possibility of running an errand for his parents. Bill is likely to say:

A. Do I have to go? Why don't you ask Uncle Joe this time?

B. Sure I'll go! Should I walk or take the bus?

C. Okay, Dad. I'll go right after I finish my homework.

D. I'm way ahead of you, Pop! I took care of it already. (Green, 1975, p. 98)

The student chose C; the correct answer was A. He explained he had chosen C because a cranky student of the sort described would not confront his father but would lie and would probably not do his homework anyway. That reasoning is much closer to the world in which I live, too. The issue here is not about cultural differences and is not about background knowledge. Nor is the issue the failure, about not understanding character. The issue is the pedagogisation of language and literacy. When I give this test to preservice or inservice teachers, they almost always get the correct answer, A, although later in discussion, they will acknowledge that C makes more sense in terms of life experience. Although they know what the test makers want, they also understand the pedagogisation of literacy.

There are numerous examples of the pedagogisation of language and literacy (for example, see Bloome, Puro, & Theodorou, 1989; Cazden, 1988; Dickens, 1854; Street & Street, 1991). The pedagogisation of language does not stop at the school door, it goes home.

Consider the recent interest in bedtime story reading and family literacy in the United States. Researchers have long claimed that parents reading to children correlates with success in school reading. Accordingly, many school districts have promoted parents reading to their children. The result in many homes has been to supplant an activity that had primarily been about developing social relationships with an academic exercise in support of schooling. In the United States, there are even television commercials encouraging bedtime story reading, because it prepares children for school and helps them achieve. The issue is not bedtime story reading itself, but rather the pedagogisation of bedtime story reading. What was once family time becomes school time with all of the meanings and social relationships identified with school. Parents become teachers, children become students. Parents who do not engage in bedtime story reading are viewed as not doing right by their children. Communities that do not have bedtime story reading as a usual practice are viewed as needing to be educated or reformed. School, as a social institution, encroaches upon and attempts to redefine the family.

Family reading has become a site of struggle over what is literacy. What was once an activity that had no definition of success or failure —parents and children either enjoyed the book they were reading or got another, either finished the book or went to sleep—now becomes an instructional activity involving success and failure. Our families, however we constitute them, are being taken away from us, supplanted by school and other social institutions.

The commodification of language

In both the United States and Britain, one can find advertisements in the daily papers for programs to improve language. I saw one in the *Guardian* (a UK newspaper) and sent for the "free" materials, receiving a booklet explaining the course called Practical English Programme. It promised to "Quickly, easily, surely...show [me] *How to earn more money—gain promotion*—by learning to express [my] ideas really well you'll impress others—promotion and higher earnings are sure to follow." Other promises included "winning friends" and "becoming popular," and claimed one would "command respect," "become more poised and self-confident," "influence others," "dominate every situation," and "think better." The booklet was filled with pictures of white men in suits seemingly discussing important business and women with notepads listening. When I did not respond, I received other discount offers.

The marketing of language and literacy education, in my view, reached a new low with the Hooked On Phonics television infomercials in the United States, which were juxtaposed with commercials for diet pills and car wax. Although the Hooked On Phonics advertisements and the language program advertised in the *Guardian* may seem obvious and overdone in their promises and commercialisation of the teaching of language, they tap into the social and economic dynamics surrounding us. Many Americans will pay large sums to lose their accent, especially if they are from the South or speak a dialect associated with people of colour (e.g., African American vernacular English) or with rural areas (e.g., so called "country" dialects). Despite a general stability or increase in literacy achievement over the past decades, newspaper headlines, and political demagogues have made parents fearful that their children are not learning to read and that teachers in general cannot be trusted to teach them. Many parents thus come to view private schools and the purchase of reading programs as insurance for school success.

The blame for the commodification of language does not lie just with commercial programs such as Hooked On Phonics or private schools. The language of education, and especially the language of assessment and evaluation, have framed language and the learning of spoken and written language in terms of "value." Some evaluations provide a list of the skills a student has acquired. Others provide analysis of the "value added" even to the point of identifying how much value specific teachers have added to their students' achievement (this practice is employed in the metropolitan Nashville, Tennessee, public schools). School administrators talk about quality control and accountability as if teaching was the same as producing tyres.

In a market economy, establishing standards is a prerequisite to fixing the value of something, otherwise how would one know its value? When educators argue over standards—should it be this standard or that one—they have accepted the premise that language is a commodity framed by a market economy.

It may appear that I am negative about business and about market economies. However, my critique is less about business and market economies per se than about the tendency of those domains to take control over other domains of life that should not be framed by business or a market economy. For example, forty years ago I collected baseball cards. Mostly I wanted the gum that came with the cards. With my friends I would flip cards, trade duplicates, and take them to baseball games. When I outgrew the cards, I gave them to my brother and, when he outgrew them, he gave them to a friend. My 11-year-old son also collects baseball cards, although there is little similarity between what he does and what I did. He regularly refers to the *Beckett* catalogue to see how much his cards are worth. He has a $10 Barry Bonds card and a $50 Sandy Koufax card among others of lesser value. He does not trade for players he likes but for players whose cards he believes will increase in value. Where I used to read the sports pages to see if the batting average listed on a player's card was going up or down, the intertextual links my son creates are between the baseball card, the sports page, and the *Beckett* catalogue to interpret the financial gain or decline of a card.

Baseball card collecting is but one of many literacy practices that have been transformed by the domains of business and a market economy. So are people. My son is not a child fantasising about being a baseball player, he is a business person speculating on commodities.

Final comments

The challenges I have briefly outlined, along with others I have not addressed, can be viewed as a struggle about how language and literacy get defined and who has the authority and power to define them. There are a series of responses to these challenges by teachers and students that seem promising, some of which are described in *Students as Researchers of Culture and Language in Their Own Communities* (in press), edited by Ann Egan-Robertson and myself (see also Walsh, 1991). The projects described in that volume do more than engage students in ethnographic and sociolinguistic research. They redefine and relocate knowledge and, in so doing, they redefine teachers and students as people acting on and in the worlds in which they live. While there is not space in this article to describe the projects, it is important to note that there is no single formula or model to follow. Although the educators who created and implemented these projects are informed by various social, cultural, sociolinguistic, and political theories, the projects reflect very close attention to the realities of people's lives and to the knowledge and language in the communities in which people live.

But these projects and similar ones aside, it seems to me that we are very far from definitions of language, and even further from a study of language—a linguistics—that does not do violence to us, to ordinary people in their everyday lives. We need definitions of language (not a single definition, but multiple definitions) that maintain all of the earthiness and high-mindedness of language, with all of its emotions and sexual energy, yet with the potential for peace and reflection. I want definitions of language that hover close to the material and everyday realities of our lives. There is nothing romantic about these realities or related definitions of language and literacy (see Street, 1996) as they are filled with the joys, pain, suffering, oppression, caring, separation, and difficulties that most of us must face. As Raymond Williams (1977) wrote, "A definition of language is always implicitly or explicitly a definition of human beings in the world."

REFERENCES

Bloome, D. (1983). Reading as a social process. In B. Hutson (Ed.), *Advances in reading/language research*, Vol. 2, (pp. 165–95). Greenwich, CT: JAI Press.

Bloome, D. (1994). You can't get there from here: An anthropological perspective on assessing children's reading and writing. In K. Holland, D. Bloome, & J.

Solsken (Eds.), *Alternative perspectives for assessing children's reading and writing*. Norwood, NJ: Ablex.

Bloome, D., Puro, P., & Theodorou, E. (1989). Procedural display and classroom lessons. *Curriculum Inquiry, 19*(3), 265–291.

Cazden, C. (1988). *Classroom discourse: The language of teaching and learning.* Portsmouth, NH: Heinemann.

Dickens, C. (1854, original). *Hard times.* Boston, MA: New Century Press.

Egan-Robertson, A., & Bloome, D. (Eds.). (In press). *Students as researchers of culture and language in their own communities.* Cresskill, NJ: Hampton Press.

Green, G. (1975). *Reading House Series: Comprehension and vocabulary.* New York: Random House.

Stierer, B., & Bloome, D. (1994). *Reading words: A commentary on key terms in the teaching of reading.* Sheffield, UK: National Association of Teachers of English.

Street, B. (1996). *Multiple literacies and multi-literacies.* Keynote address presented at Domains of Literacy Conference, Institute of Education, London, UK.

Street, J., & Street, B. (1991). The schooling of literacy. In D. Barton & R. Ivanic (Eds.), *Writing in the community.* London: Sage.

Walsh, C. (Ed.). (1991). *Literacy as Praxis: Culture, language, and pedagogy.* Norwood, NJ: Ablex.

Williams, R. (1977). *Marxism and literature.* Oxford, UK: Oxford University Press.

Willett, J., & Bloome, D. (1992). Literacy, language, school and community: A community-centered perspective. In C. Hedley & A. Carrasquillo (Eds.), *Whole language and the bilingual learner.* Norwood, NJ: Ablex.

Defining whole language in a postmodern age

Lorraine Wilson

Can whole language be "defined" in the true sense of the word? Lorraine Wilson believes that while whole language can never be defined in the sense suggested by the word's Latin root (definire = to finish, finalise), certain core principles and assumptions can be made explicit. In this article she describes how a group of whole language advocates set about defining what whole language meant for them and discusses the ten beliefs which emerged from this research.

Introduction

In a paper in the *Reading Research Quarterly* entitled "The Rhetoric of Whole Language," Moorman, Blanton, & McLaughin (1994) complain that "no concise definition of whole language exists" p. 310. Whilst they may see that this is as a problem, I don't. The very nature of whole language is that there can't be one, eternal, universal, concise definition of it. There can, however, be some consensus about it. Whole language has been broadly defined as "a set of beliefs" (Altwerger, Edelsky, & Flores, 1987), "a point of view" (Watson, 1989), "a philosophy" (Clarke, 1987; Newman & Church, 1990), or "a view of epistemology" (Pearson, 1989). Cambourne (1997) more recently defined it as "an ideology." This raises the issue of whether whole language can actually be defined in the original sense of the word, i.e. "to finish or finalise" (L. definire = to finish). The act of developing such a definition involves the construction of a knowledge system.

Scribner, DiBello, Kindred, and Zazanis (1991) have argued that knowledge systems are socially created. Lemke (1990) has argued that learning the knowledge system of a discipline or profession entails a community developing a set of shared meanings (i.e., "a language") for that discipline or profession. Thus defining something called whole language would entail a group of whole language educators reaching a sophisticated consensus of what they mean by whole language through the reading, writing, talking, and listening they do as members of such a community. This is what I set out to try to organise.

In this article, I will describe how a community of whole language educators constructed a definition of whole language that was relevant for them and their purposes. The particular community of whole language educators comprised the membership of the Teachers Applying Whole Language (TAWL) Special Interest Group of the Australian Literacy Educators' Association (ALEA)[1]. Wanting to articulate its explicit beliefs about whole language, the group posed the following two research questions:

1. What are the explicit assumptions by which this TAWL community defines itself?

2. What implicit beliefs underlie these assumptions?

In 1995 the membership was invited to submit, in writing, individual core beliefs and assumptions about whole language. The invitation was deliberately open-ended to encourage respondents to be as explicit as possible. Submissions were written by classroom teachers, university researchers, literacy consultants, and school administrators, and thus can be considered reasonably representative of Australian whole language advocates. The responses were then analysed by a sub-committee of the group. The following beliefs emerged from this analysis:

Belief 1

Whole language is a dynamic, continually growing, and evolving framework for thinking about language, learning, and literacy.

---

[1]Australian Literacy Educators' Association (ALEA). Formerly known as Australian Reading Association (ARA).

This means that: Whole language is multi-theoretical in the sense that it continually draws upon and is informed by research from many areas including psycholinguistics, sociopsycholinguistics, systemic functional linguistics, cognitive psychology, child development, genre theory, critical theory, learning theory, classroom discourse, philosophy, epistemology, praxiology, and ideology.

Belief 2

Whole language is meaning centred.

This means that: The core of whole language is the construction of appropriate and sensible meaning. No one in the real world deliberately engages in speaking, reading, or writing nonsense. We speak to mean. We write to mean. We listen to mean. We read to mean. Whole language is based on the belief that the teaching of language must occur in contexts that are meaningful for, and make sense to, every learner.

Belief 3

Whole language values the language, culture, and lives of students to empower them to take control of their lives and be critical members of their society.

This means that: Whole language teaching must start with the learners. Each child's curriculum must start with that child, with his or her language, with her or his view of the world. It cannot start with fixed language outcomes and a fixed body of knowledge prescribed in a centrally determined syllabus, which assumes children of one age are identical. Consequently, the specific details of literacy programs will differ from school to school.

For example, at Geelong Road Primary School in Footscray, Melbourne, Australia, over 90 percent of the children are of Asian origin, mainly Vietnamese. At this school, a Vietnamese teacher and Vietnamese teacher's aide use traditional Vietnamese rhymes, songs, and folk tales to provide the basis of the children's early experiences with literacy. On the other hand, children in other Australian schools may instead listen to Dreamtime stories in their first year of school. Such stories would not have the same meaning for children at Geelong Road, Footscray, and vice versa. Then again, the children of Moonee Ponds West Primary School are predominantly middle-class Anglo children. Neither the Dreamtime stories of the Aboriginal culture nor the Vietnamese rhymes and songs provide a bridge between pre-school literacy and school literacy for these children in the way that popular picture storybooks do.

While whole language teachers value literacy as a medium for personal growth and development, they are predominantly concerned with literacy for social equity. They view language as a cultural resource, and believe that access to power and equity in our culture is contingent upon control of many forms of language. They, therefore, aim to create classrooms which support learners in the acquisition of the skills and knowledge necessary for understanding the links between language and status and language and power.

Belief 4

We learn language, we learn through language, and we learn about language simultaneously as we use it.

This means that: Whole language teachers believe students are best able to learn about language as a by-product of using it to meet their social and cognitive needs. It is the opposite of believing that we first of all need to be taught language and, then after we've been taught it, we can be taught *about* it.

Belief 5

Whole language views listening, speaking, reading, and writing as integrated, not separate domains.

This means that: Whole language teachers treat reading, writing, speaking, and listening as parallel forms of the same thing, namely, language. They further believe that each of these forms of language can both feed off and feed into each other and that this feeding is what increases each person's total pool of language. Thus they understand the link between reading and writing and the way that reading nourishes writing and vice versa. Whole language teaching builds upon the relationships between listening, speaking, reading, and writing.

Belief 6

Whole language recognises that an individual learner's knowledge is socially constructed through collaboration with others.

This means that: Whole language teachers value co-operative learning as children share, ask questions, hypothesise, compromise, argue, report, draw conclusions, teach, and much more. Whole language teachers value the negotiated understandings that develop as children talk and work together. They also acknowledge that each child is active in constructing meanings through interactions with others, and that because of different life experiences, each learner's perceptions will vary. They encourage children to ask questions, offer interpretations, challenge other children's beliefs, and follow hunches. Because of all this, many whole language teachers favour multi-age classes. Finally, whole language means that competition is not highly valued.

Belief 7

Whole language acknowledges and recognises the relationship between text, context, and linguistic choice.

This means that: Whole language teachers understand that context changes according to the subject matter, the purpose, and the audience for the communication. As the context changes so do the linguistic choices. Language is always used for a purpose and has an audience. Purpose and audience mutually shape the text, and thus determine the genre.

Belief 8

Whole language recognises that students are active participants in their learning.

This means that: Whole language teachers view language learning as a form of hypothesis testing. Children form hypotheses about how language works. They try out these hypotheses while actually using language. With further experience they test and refine them, forming rules or generalisations. These personal hypotheses are refined according to the social conventions of the language community of which the individual is a member.

Belief 9

Whole language recognises that students learn the subsystems of language as they engage in whole language use. It is only while students are using language that the teacher can observe the students' control of subsystems, the needs they may have, and plan the appropriate strategies.

This means that: Whole language teachers understand that language is a series of subsystems (phonemic, graphic, syntactic, semantic, pragmatic), which all interact together to create meaning simultaneously. They recognise that students best learn the subsystems of language (e.g., phonics, syntax, punctuation) as they engage in whole language use. Furthermore they understand that phonics, the meaningful and explicit teaching of sound-letter patterns, is an integral part of whole language.

It also means that whole language teachers do not "sit back and let it happen." A whole language classroom is not a laissez-faire environment. Every time a whole language teacher plans a demonstration, she is intervening. Every time a whole language teacher responds to an individual child's writing at conference time, he is intervening. Every time a whole language teacher makes explicit the invisible processes of reading, writing, spelling, and thinking, she is intervening. Every time a teacher demands that students clarify their intent, every time a teacher refocusses, redirects, or modifies their learning, he is intervening.

Belief 10

Whole language recognises that teachers are professionals who are life-long learners

This means that: Whole language teachers are perpetual learners. They learn by observing students closely. They learn from each other. They learn by engaging in ongoing professional development. Whole language teachers are therefore able to articulate and develop their beliefs and make informed curriculum decisions which are responsive to the needs of the students they teach.

Conclusion

In the introduction to this article, I alluded to the issue of whether whole language can actually be defined in the original sense of the word, i.e. to finish or finalise. I am convinced that while I have been able to describe (define) those beliefs common to a group of Australian whole language educators at this time, this set of beliefs will not remain static. I would expect that as we learn more about language and learning, and as society changes, this same community will also change its beliefs, and thus its definition.

REFERENCES

Altwerger, B., Edelsky, C., & Flores, B. (1987). Whole language: What's new? *The Reading Teacher, 41*, 144–154.

Cambourne, B. (1997). Ideology and the teaching of phonics: An Australian perspective. In A. Marek & C. Edelsky (Eds.), *A Festschrift for Kenneth Goodman.* New York, NY: Macmillan.

Clarke, M. (1987). Don't blame the system: Constraints on whole language reform. *Language Arts, 64*, 384–396.

Lemke, J. (1990). *Talking science.* Norwood, NJ: Ablex.

Moorman, G., Blanton, W., & McLaughlin, T. (1994). The rhetoric of whole language. *Reading Research Quarterly, 29*, 308–329.

Newman, J., & Church, S. (1990). Myths of whole language. *The Reading Teacher, 44*, 20–26.

Pearson, P. (1989). Reading the whole language movement. *The Elementary School Journal, 90*, 231–241.

Scribner, S., DiBello, L., Kindred, J., & Zazanis, E. (1991). *Coordinating two knowledge systems: A case study.* New York: New York Laboratory for Cognitive Studies of Work, City University of New York.

Watson, D. (1989). Defining and describing whole language. *The Elementary School Journal, 90*, 129–141.

Towards a personal theory of whole language: A teacher-researcher-writer reflects

Mem Fox

In this article, children's author and university teacher Mem Fox puts on her reflective practitioner's hat and makes explicit her personal theory of whole language.

Most people regard me primarily as an author. I prefer to think of myself as a teacher-researcher who sometimes writes children's books.

My research takes a number of forms. There are the observations I make and the conversations I have in the classes I teach at university and in the schools and classrooms in which I work as a teacher educator. Then there are the thousands of letters I receive from readers of my books and the hundreds of pieces of writing my students and I produce.

I analyse these data by engaging in what Guba and Lincoln (1989) describe as "the hermeneutic dialectic process" (p. 149). Put simply, this means that I am constantly:

- reading what others are writing about literacy;
- discussing my own experiences, observations, and conclusions with professional peers, students I teach, and children who read my books;
- reflecting on and writing about my own and others' interpretations of literacy; and
- refining what I know, believe, and understand.

As a researcher, I guess I'm a cross between a "reflective practitioner" (Schon, 1983), an "action researcher" (Kemmis & McTaggert, 1982), and a "participant observer" (Bogdan & Biklen, 1982). I'm glad

I've managed to be such a hybrid. It's helped me grow professionally, to keep my thoughts moving. Consequently, over the last fifteen years, my perceptions of whole language have evolved and changed. This article summarises my new thinking.

A personal theory of whole language

For me, whole language is neither a method, nor a philosophy, nor an approach, although it has overtones of each of these. It is a framework comprising one assumption and nine principles.

An assumption

There are factors apparent which apply to anything that we need or want to learn. They are not limited to, but are particularly obvious in, language acquisition. Children learn to talk before they come to school. We know that. We've heard it ad nauseam for the last twenty years (Cambourne, 1988, 1995; Smith, 1988). No one appears to teach them. They learn, without much effort, without much failure, without worksheets, without comprehension exercises in how to talk and listen, without weekly tests to see how they're getting on, without set assignments, without essays, and without exams. In an ordinary household, therefore, "right things" must be happening. I believe these right things can be expressed as basic principles.

Nine principles

Relationships

In an ordinary household, the relationships between young children and older members of a family make it easy for a child to learn to talk. Young learners bond with and are supported by older family members. They can take risks without fear (Haas-Dyson, 1989; Parkes, 1990).

When we aim to develop literacy, we need first to establish good relationships in our classrooms, so that our students feel safe enough to learn without fear, so they won't be afraid to take risks. If there's no bond between the learner and the teacher and between the learners themselves, there'll be less efficient learning.

Relationships are fundamental to learning. Teachers cannot be aloof, detached, or apolitical. We cannot withhold personal information, keep our first name a secret, pretend to have no emotions, or merely feign interest in children's worlds. We must interact honestly with our students. Real life literacy is always a social event, so our classrooms need that scaffold of social cohesion.

Immersion

Babies are typically surrounded by talk. They're bombarded by it. They can't get away from it. There's no escape. It's talk, talk, talk, all day long.

When we develop literacy, we should be reading aloud daily, bombarding children with the best texts available. The educational ramifications of hearing literature read aloud are so positive there can never be too much of it (Holdaway, 1979). We need our classroom shelves to be crammed with trade books, comics, magazines, newspapers, journals, and catalogues, so our students are offered a variety of reading and writing options.

Although immersion is the principle most advocates of whole language understand, my data suggest that there is not nearly enough reading aloud from kindergarten through college level. Some students go for weeks and sometimes years without ever hearing writing read aloud. Others are read aloud to so badly that the positives become negatives.

Demonstration

Normally, children witness millions of demonstrations of language in use (Holdaway, 1979). They're exposed to jokes, plans, arguments, requests, questions, complaints, stories, endearments, advertisements, songs, explanations, and so on. Through these demonstrations, they come to understand what talk is and what it achieves. No wonder they want to do it!

My data show that this principle is poorly understood by some teachers. Demonstration is so important, so crucial to learning, that it ought to have a sizzling place in our programs. Unfortunately, it's on the back burner or even in a cold oven in some classrooms. It's a serious misconception that whole language teachers do not teach. Demonstration *is* teaching. Teaching is a guided tour around demonstrations.

The question is not *whether* to teach spelling, phonics, punctuation, paragraphing, grammar, and structure: it's *when* and *how* we teach them. Of course they have to be taught! Children need to be taught them over and over again. They need to be shown explicitly the elements of any genre they are about to use (Derewianka, 1990; Hammond, 1990), as well as being provided with words that describe the elements of style and writing such as noun, verb, exclamation mark, inverted commas, lead, showing-not-telling, and so on. It's too hard to learn anything without the guided tour around the demonstration.

Why have some teachers stopped teaching things like spelling? I think they heard statements such as "You don't do spelling lists in whole language," so they stopped teaching spelling altogether. It was the wrong message. We must teach spelling. We all need the power of being able to spell correctly. I teach spelling by having minilessons. I play word games. I have guided tours around the complexities of words that end in *ough*, or *tion*, or *ck*. I have lists of those word patterns on charts hanging from the ceiling in sentences that are meaningful to my students:

It's *tough* being in the classroom on such a great day.

Mum said, "*Enough* is enough" when I asked for another dog.

I don't like the *rough* hands of my grandfather.

Later I say, "Look, that list is fine for the spelling, but the sentences don't relate to each other, do they? They have no connected meaning. They're a sort of non-sense, right? You have ten minutes in your groups to write a news item (we would have interrogated the news item genre, of course), which includes and connects those words. Your aim this time is to shock us. Off you go!"

It's fun, there's a purpose, an audience, and an expected response. If the spelling we teach is within writing that has meaning for our students, it's fine to have entire lessons where we do nothing but spelling.

Ditto phonics. I once heard a teacher say, "Oh, I'm a whole language teacher now. I don't do phonics any more." How did she imagine her class was going to learn to read? By osmosis? While immersion and exposure are essential, they aren't enough. Children need help sorting out sound-symbol relationships. If an explicit knowledge of phonics is essential in learning to read, how can we teach it?

Certainly not through worksheets that have no meaning. Our aim is to create what I call "a climate of vital curiosity," to instil in our students a fascination about individual words, their component parts, their letters, and the way those letters sound by reading aloud from Big Books, by singing songs and following the words, by chorally speaking well-loved poems and chants, and by engaging in group writing activities. We need to teach, that is we need to demonstrate, until we drop.

My data strongly suggest that phonic skills are best learned by allowing children to create their own meanings through writing. If they have to grapple with the sounds and letters of print in an attempt to communicate with others, they'll be teaching themselves phonics faster than we can ever teach it to them.

Needs and purposes: The "investment" or reality factor

A child won't talk unless there's a need to talk. This is the "What's in it for me?" factor. Children learn to talk out of a desperate need to do so.

Potty! Potty!

Me want onjooce.

Mine!

They do not talk unless there's something in it for them.

When we teach English, we must create real reasons for reading and writing by writing letters, poems, jokes, directions, explanations, stories, histories, laws, protest notes, posters, advertisements, recipes, science experiments, for someone—not for no one—either for quiet publication (silent reading by others) or to share aloud. Writers care about writing which has a purpose and an audience. They care about the organisation and clear meaning, about spelling, grammar, and punctuation. Writing without purpose and audience means writing without caring, writing without improvement (Fox, 1993).

The same applies to learning to read. If they don't receive deep satisfaction from reading, children will rightly think: What's in it for me?

Nothing! So why should I try? We need to create a real purpose for and investment in reading.

Expectation

As Cambourne has pointed out, parents and the rest of the family do not question the fact that their baby will eventually learn to talk (Cambourne 1988, 1995). Success is taken for granted.

When we aim to develop literacy, we should remember to expect success in reading and writing. We must assume that if we reach for the stars our students will be able to grab them.

I have a hunch that our belief in children's abilities is sinking. We're worried that they won't be able to learn because of attention deficit disorder, poverty, Aboriginality, having a single parent, being a second language learner, and so on. What we expect from students is what we will receive, which is why we should aim for the stars, not the mud.

I also feel that we praise too often, and too much, work that's mediocre. I know I sometimes do to encourage students, but ultimately it isn't helpful. Much of what many students write is piddlingly pathetic for people of their age. A little real criticism will raise the standard because the students will know we care; and they'll understand that we know and they know that they can do better. Of course, we can be critical only if we have the right relationships operating in our classrooms.

Approximation

The sixth principle can be passed over very quickly. It's been one of the clearest messages of whole language: Let children know that no one's perfect the first time around. We let them have a go. We allow them the decision-making power to draft first and refine later.

We know that no one's perfect the first time around, because we've noticed that in any ordinary household, new attempts at meaning making are often hilariously inept. Nevertheless, they are greeted with joy. Parents are so excited when their child manages to say something as deeply unexciting as "Doggie all don! Where doggie don?" that they ring up grandparents to boast about it. They take notice of what their child *can* do, not what he or she can't do, and they enthuse, and praise, and rave like lunatics so the child feels proud and is encouraged to continue to learn.

When we teach we should strive to do likewise: to rave like lunatics. We should rejoice in invented spelling when our students are young. The following letter isn't perfect, but it's almost there. This very young writer can certainly communicate.

> Dear Mrs. Fox,
>
> I like you name because you last name is fox and I like nice foxes. Are you marled? I don't know if you are. I midov put the rong thing. Do you like my name? I like youis.
>
> Love,
> Summer

If, however, our students are still inventing spelling at the age of nine (or even nineteen), they clearly need a real reason for their writing so they care about getting the spelling right.

Response

Typically, toddlers don't speak to the wall, because the wall won't reply. All real communication entails someone making meaning and then having it reciprocated. When a toddler says something it's to a real person for a real response. On rare occasions the response is a direct correction, as in "It's *drowned*, not *drownded*, stupid." Most often, however, the response is to the meaning the child is trying to make. "Me done poohs," gets the response: "Oh, you smelly thing. Come here and let me change your nappy." Imagine a mother saying instead: "You mean, I have done a bowel motion in my napkin. Now say it again properly, after me."

Although it is important to respond genuinely to the meaning attempted in any piece of writing before we criticise the mechanics, some of the responses I've seen are very weak. Too often they are generic and fatuous: "This is a lovely piece of work. I enjoyed it very much." Responses must be more encouraging and have more bite and focus. A writer longs for a full response. We have to respond in ways that prove we have read the offering:

This is a savagely effective piece. I loved it even though it was so depressing. The first paragraph made me laugh so much I thought it was going to be funny all the way through, but you really socked it to me from paragraph two onwards. I've been thinking about the message about dads in general, and mine in particular, ever since. If you can, I'd like you to read this to the class on Father's Day, even though it's not for a few months yet.

By the way, *dad* needs a capital only when it's used as a proper noun, not when it's a common noun. The metaphor in the last line is stunning. Treasure this piece. We all need to hear it.

Showing a real interest in the meaning of a piece of writing is the first requirement from any reader to any writer. Criticism of errors in structure should not be forgotten, because teaching correct spelling is an essential principle of whole language. It shouldn't, however, take precedence over meaning.

Refinement

The penultimate factor is refinement: drafting until it's right, or practicing spoken language until we're understood, or re-reading until we get the right meaning.

Young children's meaning making is often unclear. Puzzled parents respond in ways that tell children whether their meaning is or isn't clear.

When we teach we ought to allow opportunity for self-correction and refinement, by providing both honest responses and demonstrations, particularly when meaning is unclear, information is left out, we're bored, or confused. We should try to provide our students with the conditions real writers need—time to make mistakes, to be messy, to re-draft, and to be edited, if necessary, by others.

Refinement is not being well done. I'm still seeing too many pieces of writing which are marvellous examples of approximation but poor examples of refinement. It's fine for Kindergarten, Year 1, and Year 2 children to have invented spelling and lack of cohesion in their final drafts. But beyond that (for most learners), surely we can explain that there are standards or politenesses that have been developed to help make meaning clear to our readers, and that we have to meet those standards in any piece that goes public. It shouldn't be a great drama to demand of our students better spelling and punctuation, structure, and style, so long as we bring in those good old expectations and make writing significant for children by providing real purposes and responses and as many demonstrations as possible.

We can save time on the re-drafting of writing by helping children to learn certain words before they start. It's unnecessary to have thirty different invented spellings for *favourite* in thirty letters from one class.

My farit book ov yous is psm majeck.

Is you favrit book Cwaleloo?

Kwili Lou is my fart bk.

Wouldn't it be more sensible to teach the spelling of words that students will need by writing *Koala Lou* and *favourite* on the board and then creating a climate of curiosity about those words to fix them in children's minds?

Celebration

Celebration is the final principle. Why celebrate? Typically, when a child takes a first step, repeats a rhyme, or says something cute like, "I wuv you, Daddy," adults go wild and want the child to do it again. There are claps and cheers and kisses—reactions which give the child the encouragement to excel even further.

When we teach we need celebrations. Writing and reading achievements can be lauded by framing, fridge decoration, publishing, sharing, and performing—to amaze children with their own capabilities. Celebrations create a willingness to continue learning. Special days lift the spirits, renew ambition, and help set new goals.

If we want whole language to be our chosen framework for teaching, we need to remember that it can only be successful if all nine principles are adhered to. We have to teach, and we have to do much more than teach. We have to set up situations in which there exist all of the fabulous factors for language learning:

Relationships

Immersion

Demonstration

Needs and Purposes

Expectation

Approximation

Purpose

Response

Refinement

Celebration

If even one of these is absent, literacy teaching will be neither efficient nor effective. Now we wouldn't want *that*, would we?

REFERENCES

Bogdan, R., & Biklen, S. (1982). *Qualitative research for education: An introduction to theory and methods*. Needham Heights, MA: Allyn & Bacon.

Cambourne, B. (1988). *The whole story: Natural learning and the acquisition of literacy*. Auckland, NZ: Ashton Scholastic.

Cambourne, B. (1995). Toward an educationally relevant theory of learning: Twenty years of inquiry. *The Reading Teacher, 49*, 182–190.

Derewianka, B. (1990). *Exploring how texts work*. Rozelle, NSW: Primary English Teaching Association.

Fox, M. (1993). *Radical reflections*. Sydney, NSW: Harcourt Brace.

Guba, E., & Lincoln, Y. (1989). *Fourth generation evaluation*. Thousand Oaks, CA: Sage.

Haas-Dyson, A. (1989). The space/time travels of story writers. *Language Arts, 66*, 330–340.

Hammond, J. (1990). Is learning to read and write the same as learning to speak? In F. Chrtistie (Ed.), *Literacy for a changing world*. Hawthorn, Victoria: Australian Council of Education Research.

Holdaway, D. (1979). *The foundations of literacy*. Gosford, NSW: Ashton.

Kemmis, S., & McTaggert, R. (1982). *The action research planner*. Geelong, Victoria: Deakin University Press.

Parkes, B. (1990). *Case study explorations of emergent literacy learners' transactions with picture story books*. Unpublished doctoral thesis, University of Wollongong, NSW, Australia.

Schon, D. (1983). *The reflective practitioner: How professionals think in action*. New York: Basic Books.

Smith, F. (1988). *Joining the literacy club*. London: Heinemann.

Teaching factual writing: Purpose and structure

David Wray and Maureen Lewis

These two researchers from the United Kingdom remind us of the need to focus on the teaching of factual texts in primary classrooms. They offer one particular teaching strategy, "writing frames," trialed by teachers in the Exeter Extending Literacy (EXEL) project, as a useful strategy in assisting young writers learn to write factual texts.

Introduction

As members of a postmodern literate society, we need to read and write a wide range of texts, including factual texts. However, much of the research in the United Kingdom into the development of children's writing has concentrated on personal and fictional texts while factual literacy has been relatively neglected. Our work with teachers in the Exeter Extending Literacy (EXEL) project (see, for example, Lewis, Wray, & Rospigliosi, 1994) demonstrated that although many classroom practitioners recognised the need to widen the range and quality of children's non-fiction writing they were unsure as to how to do this. This article sets out to describe the theoretical background to our project and some of its practical outcomes.

Genre theory: New insights, new approaches

There has been an increasing interest in encouraging students to write for a particular purpose, for a known audience, and in an appropriate form. However, what constitutes an appropriate form is often presented in general lists of different text types; for example, "notes, letters, in-structions, stories, and poems, in order to plan, inform, explain, entertain, and express attitudes or emotions" (Department of Education and Science, 1990).

Such lists imply that teachers and students know what differentiates one text type from another. At one level this may be true—we all know that a story or narrative usually has a beginning, a series of events, and an ending. We have a general sense that this differs from a recipe. And many teachers discuss these differences with their students. However, it is still relatively rare, in the UK anyway, for teachers of elementary school students to discuss non-fiction texts by drawing on knowledge of the usual structure of a particular text type in order to improve students' writing.

It has been argued (e.g., Martin, 1985) that our implicit knowledge of text types and their forms is quite extensive, and one of the teacher's roles is to make this implicit knowledge explicit. Theorists in this area have been referred to as "genre theorists," and they base their work on a functional approach to language (Halliday, 1985). They see all texts, written and spoken, as being "produced in a response to, and out of, particular social situations and their specific structures" (Kress & Knapp, 1992, p. 5) and, as a result, put stress on the social and cultural factors that form a text as well as on its linguistic features. They view a text as a social object and the making of a text as a social process. They argue that in any society there are certain types of text—both written and spoken—of a particular form, because there are similar social encounters and events which recur constantly within that society. As these events are repeated over and over again certain types of text are created over and over again. These texts become recognised by the members of a society and, once recognised, they become conventionalised, i.e. become distinct genres.

These distinct genres, however, need to be learned by our children. And we need to help to make explicit the purpose and features of such genres for them.

Written genres in the classroom

Several ways of categorising the written genres used in classrooms have been proposed over the years. Collerson (1988) categorises written genres into early genres (labels, observational comment, recount, and narratives) and factual genres (procedural, reports, explanations, and arguments or exposition), while Wing Jan's (1991) categories are factual genres (reports, explanations, procedures, persuasive writing, interviews, surveys, descriptions, biographies, recounts, and narrative information) and fictional genres (traditional fiction and contemporary modern fiction).

In our project, we took as our model the categories of non-fiction genres identified by linguists Martin and Rothery (1980, 1981, 1986). The six non-fiction genres they identified were recount, report, procedure, explanation, argument, and discussion. Of these, recount was overwhelmingly the most used in student writing.

Martin and Rothery argue that being competent in the use of non-fiction written genres in our society offers the language user access to power. Persuasion, explanation, report, explanation, and discussion are powerful forms of language that we use to get things done and, thus, have been labelled the "language of power." It can be argued that students who leave our classrooms unable to operate successfully within these powerful genres are denied access to becoming fully functioning members of society. This suggests we can no longer accept the overwhelming dominance of recount in our students' non-fiction writing. Our challenge as teachers is to provide students with the language of power.

The problems of writing non-fiction

For the inexperienced writer this overuse of "written down talk" or written recount can indicate a lack of knowledge about the differences between speech and written language.

Bereiter and Scardamalia (1987) highlight the supportive, prompting nature of conversation where somebody speaks, which prompts someone else to say something and so on. This reciprocal prompting or turn taking is missing from the interaction between a writer and a blank sheet of paper. Bereiter and Scardamalia's research has shown that a teacher's oral promptings during writing can extend a student's written work, with no drop in quality. The prompts act as an "external trigger of discourse production" (p. 97). The teacher-student and peer conferences have become part of writing classrooms, it would seem, to support this process. Bereiter and Scardamalia further suggest that students need to "acquire a functional substitute for...an encouraging listener."

Other problems students experience when reading and writing non-fiction text are caused by the complexity of the cohesive ties used, the use of more formal registers, and the use of technical vocabulary (Anderson & Armbruster, 1981; Halliday & Hasan, 1976; Perera, 1984).

An approach to helping students

Our challenge was to find ways of supporting students in their learning to write non-fiction. Vygotsky proposed that children first experience a particular cognitive activity in collaboration with expert practitioners. The child is firstly a spectator as the majority of the cognitive work is done by the expert (usually a parent or a teacher), then a novice as he or she starts to take over while under the close supervision of the expert. As the child grows in experience and capability of performing the task, the expert passes over greater and greater responsibility but still acts as a guide, assisting the child at problematic points. Eventually, the child assumes full responsibility for the task with the expert still present in the role of a supportive audience. This model fits what is known theoretically about teaching and learning. It is also a model which is familiar to teachers who have adopted such teaching strategies as paired reading and an apprenticeship approach. An adaptation of this model to the teaching of writing can be seen in Figure 1.

Figure 1   An apprenticeship model of teaching writing

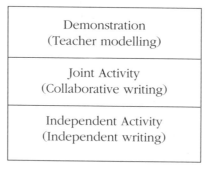

In busy, over-populated classrooms, however, it can be difficult to use this model, constructed around an ideal of a child and an expert working together on a one-to-one basis, as a guide to practical teaching action. In particular, it seems that students are too often expected to move into the independent writing phase before they are ready. Often the pressure to do so is based on the practical problem of teachers being unable to find the time to spend with them in individual support. What is clearly needed is something to span the Joint Activity and Independent Activity phases.

We proposed a scaffolded phase, where we offer our students strategies to aid writing but strategies that they can use without an adult necessarily being alongside them (see Figure 2).

One such strategy we have been exploring is that of *writing frames*. A writing frame consists of a skeleton outline to scaffold students' non-fiction writing. The skeleton framework consists of different key words or phrases, according to the particular genre. The template of starters, connectives, and sentence modifiers which constitute a writing frame gives students a structure within which they can concentrate on communicating what they want to say while scaffolding them in the use of a particular genre. And, in the process of using the genre, students become increasingly familiar with it. The frame should be developed with the students drawing on how the various non-fiction genres are structured in what they read.

Figure 2   A revised apprenticeship model of teaching writing

| Demonstration (Teacher modelling) |
| Joint Activity (Collaborative writing) |
| Scaffolded Activity (Supported writing) |
| Independent Activity (Independent writing) |

How writing frames can help

The work of Cairney (1990) on story frames and Cudd and Roberts (1989) on "expository paragraph frames" first suggested to us that children's early attempts at written structures might profitably be scaffolded. Cairney describes story frames as "a form of probed text recall" and a "story level cloze," whilst Cudd and Roberts claim that expository frames "provide a bridge which helps ease the transition from narrative to content area reading and writing." Using these as a model to develop frames that would introduce students to a wider range of genres, we have evolved and developed, in collaboration with teachers, a range of writing frames for use in the classroom. These frames have been widely used with children throughout the elementary and middle school years and across the full range of abilities, including students with special needs. On the strength of this extensive trialling, we are confident in saying that not only do writing frames help students become familiar with unfamiliar genres but that they also help overcome many of the other problems often associated with non-fiction writing.

There are many possible frames for each genre and we have space here for only two examples (see Lewis & Wray, 1995; and Lewis and Wray, 1996, for much more extensive discussion).

Recount genre

Using the recount frame given in Figure 3, nine-year-old Rachel wrote about her trip to Plymouth Museum (Figure 4). The frame helped structure her writing and allowed her to make her own sense of what she had seen. It encouraged her to reflect upon her learning.

Figure 3   A recount frame

Although I already knew that . . . .
I have learnt some new facts. I learnt that . . . .
I also learnt that . . . .
Another fact I learnt was . . . .
However the most interesting thing I learnt was . . . .

Figure 4   Rachel's framed recount

A trip to Plymouth Museum

Although I already knew that they buried their dead in mummy cases I was surprised that the paint stayed on for all these years. I have learnt some new facts. I learnt that the River Nile had a god called Hopi. He was in charge of the River Nile and he brought the floods. I also learnt that sometimes people carried a little charm so you tell a lie and you rubbed the charm's tummy and it would be OK. Another fact I learnt was that they put pretend scarab beetles on their hair for decoration. However the most interesting thing I learnt was they mummified cats and sometimes mice as well.

Discussion genre

Using the discussion frame in Figure 5 helped eleven-year-old Kerry write a thoughtful discussion about boxing (Figure 6). The frame encouraged her to structure the discussion to look at both sides of the argument.

How the frames might be used

The use of a frame should always begin with discussion and teacher modelling before moving on to joint construction (teacher and students together) and then to the student undertaking writing supported by the frame. This oral, teacher-modelling, joint construction pattern of teaching is vital, for it not only models the generic form and teaches the words that signal connections and transitions but it also provides opportunities for developing students' oral language and their thinking. Some students, especially those with learning difficulties, may need many oral sessions and sessions in which their teacher acts as a scribe before they are ready to attempt their own framed writing.

It would be useful for teachers to make "big" versions of the frames for use in these teacher-modelling and joint-construction phases. These large frames can be used for shared writing. It is important that the child and the teacher understand that the frame is a supportive draft and that words may be crossed out or substituted, extra sentences may be added, or surplus starters crossed out.

Figure 5   A discussion frame

There is a lot of discussion about whether ....
The people who agree with this idea, such as ....
claim that ....
They also argue that ....
A further point they make is ....
However there are also strong arguments against this point of view.
.... believe that ....
Another counter argument is ....
Furthermore ....
After looking at the different points of view and the evidence for them I think
.... because ....

Figure 6   Kerry's framed discussion

There is a lot of discussion about whether boxing should be banned. The people who agree with this idea, such as Sarah, claim that if they do carry on boxing they should wear something to protect their heads. They also argue that people who do boxing could have brain damage and get seriously hurt. A further point they make is that most of the people that have died did have families.

However, there are also strong arguments against this point of view. Another group of people believe that boxing should not be banned. They say that why did they invent it if it is a dangerous sport. They say that boxing is a good sport, people enjoy it. A furthermore reason is if this a good sport, people enjoy it. A furthermore reason is if they ban boxing it will ruin people's careers.

After looking at the different points of view and the evidence for them I think boxing should be banned.

We are convinced that writing in a range of genres is most effective if it is located in meaningful experiences. The concept of "situated learning" (Lave & Wenger, 1991) suggests that learning is always context-dependent. Thus, we have always used the frames within class topic or theme work rather than in isolated study skills lessons (Lewis & Wray, 1995).

We do not advocate using the frames for the direct teaching of generic structures in skills-centred lessons. The frame itself is never a purpose for writing. Our use of a writing frame has always arisen from students having a purpose for undertaking some writing, and the appropriate frame was then introduced if they needed extra help.

We have found the frames helpful to students of all ages and all abilities (and, indeed, their wide applicability is one of their most positive features). Teachers have commented on the improved quality (and quantity) of writing that has resulted from using the frames with their students.

It would, of course, be unnecessary to use a frame with writers already confident and fluent in a particular genre, but they can be used to introduce such writers to new genres. Teachers have noted an initial dip in the quality of the writing when comparing the framed new genre writing with the fluent recount writing of an able child. What they have later discovered, however, is that, after only one or two uses of a frame, fluent language users add the genre and its language features into their repertoires and, without using a frame, produce fluent writing of high quality in that genre.

The aim with all students is for them to reach this stage of assimilating the generic structures and language features into their writing repertoires. Use of writing frames should be focussed on particular children or small group of students as and when they need them.

Conclusion

We need to give greater attention to teaching students to write effective and well-structured non-fiction texts. The concept of genre gives a useful framework, while writing frames are a strategy that helps us help students to reach our goals.

REFERENCES

Anderson, T., & Armbruster, B. (1981). *Content area textbooks* (Reading Education Report No. 24). Champaign-Urbana, IL: University of Illinois, Center for the Study of Reading.

Bereiter, C., & Scardamalia, M. (1987). *The psychology of written composition*. Hillsdale, NJ: Erlbaum.

Cairney, T. (1990). *Teaching reading comprehension*. Milton Keynes, UK: Open University Press.

Collerson, J. (1988). *Writing for life*. Newtown, NSW: Primary English Teaching Association.

Cudd, E., & Roberts, L. (1989). Using writing to enhance content area learning in the primary grades. *The Reading Teacher, 42*(6), 392–404.

Department of Education and Science. (1990). *English in the national curriculum*. London: HMSO.

Halliday, M. (1985). *An introduction to functional grammar*. London: Arnold.

Halliday, M., & Hasan, R. (1976). *Cohesion in English*. London: Longman.

Kress, G., & Knapp, P. (1992). Genre in a social theory of language. *English in Education, 26*(2).

Lave, J., & Wenger, E. (1991). *Situated learning*. Cambridge, UK: Cambridge University Press.

Lewis, M., & Wray, D. (1995). *Developing children's non-fiction writing*. Leamington Spa, UK: Scholastic.

Lewis, M., & Wray, D. (1996). *Writing frames*. Reading, UK: Reading and Language Information Centre, University of Reading.

Lewis, M., Wray, D., & Rospigliosi, P. (1994). "...And I want it in your own words." *The Reading Teacher, 47*(7), 528–536.

Martin, J. (1985). *Factual writing: Exploring and challenging social reality*. Oxford, UK: Oxford University Press.

Martin, J., & Rothery, J. (1980). *Writing Project Report No. 1*. Sydney, NSW: Department of Linguistics, University of Sydney.

Martin, J., & Rothery, J. (1981). *Writing Project Report No. 2*. Sydney, NSW: Department of Linguistics, University of Sydney.

Martin, J. & Rothery, J. (1986). *Writing Project Report No. 4*. Sydney, NSW: Department of Linguistics, University of Sydney.

Perera, K. (1984). *Children's reading and writing*. Oxford, UK: Blackwell.

Wing Jan, L. (1991). *Write ways: Modelling writing forms*. Melbourne, Victoria: Oxford University Press.

They don't teach spelling anymore—or do they?

Chrystine Bouffler

Spelling has been a contentious issue for as long as there have been schools. In this article Bouffler argues that whole language teachers do teach spelling. She clearly explains where spelling fits within the postmodern whole language classroom, thus providing evidence and support for whole language teachers.

How often have you heard it on talk-back radio, TV, in casual conversation, or read it in the newspapers? "They don't teach spelling anymore!" Such assertions are usually accompanied by claims of declining standards and reflections on past methods of teaching as though there was an ideal educational era when all students left school being able to read, write, and spell. More often than not, the method under attack is an approach called "whole language." Unfortunately, few media critics understand the approach and tend to use the label to apply to a variety of teaching approaches with which they disagree.

Spelling has been a contentious issue for centuries. The debate over standards and teaching methods is as old as public education itself. Issues of standards are extremely complex, although often presented as simple, and while it is important that these complexities be recognised, they are not within the scope of this article. It suffices to say that we live in a very different world with different demands and different understandings from those that pertained when most teachers went to school. What is taught in spelling and how it is taught in a postmodern society is, and has to be, different from the way spelling was taught in a previous era. The fact that spelling is not taught as it once was, especially by teachers of whole language, does not mean that it is not taught. I wish to assert unequivocally that teachers who understand whole language do teach spelling.

Whole language: What is it?

Much of what passes as whole language is questionable. Many teachers think that because they employ strategies which appear to be whole language, such as using children's books in their reading program, encouraging proofreading, and publishing children's writing, they are doing something called whole language. But unless such strategies are consistent with a set of understandings about language, learning, and curriculum which permeate all teaching, teachers are not using a whole language approach at all.

Whole language is not simply a teaching method, and so no two whole language classrooms are alike. Nor are the thinking and views of any two whole language theorists. They too develop their understandings in different ways. Nevertheless, they all operate from a set of shared principles. Put briefly, these include:

- Although written language differs from spoken language both are forms of the same thing.
- Language is for making meaning and accomplishing purposes.
- All language is contextual and contexts affect meaning.
- Not only do language users construct meaning they are also constructed by language.
- Language is best learned in meaningful and purposeful situations.

Whole language and spelling

What critics usually mean by the claim that whole language teachers do not teach spelling is that they do not teach spelling lists in their traditional sense. Most people making this claim were brought up on the regular weekly spelling list and spelling test and, if they were successful, attribute their success to this. In the past, teachers collected written work and regularly marked out spelling and grammatical errors.

Because critics do not see these practices in evidence they assume that spelling is not being taught. Simply arguing that whole language teachers teach spelling through reading and writing and that the correction of spelling and grammatical errors is seen as the responsibility of the writer is hardly likely to silence critics. While some explanation is necessary, it should be emphasised that what follows is *a* whole language view, not *the* whole language view.

English orthography

While agreeing with Yule (1995) that there is scope for the reform of English spelling, it is also true that the English system of orthography is not as chaotic as many would believe. It might make it easier for writers if there were a direct one-to-one correspondence between sounds and symbols, but this would make it more difficult for readers. Pronunciation, the most unstable aspect of language, varies greatly from country to country or even within countries. Despite this, English standard written form can be read regardless of where it was generated. It is not only sound that is represented by the orthography but semantic and syntactic units as well, because this makes it easier for the reader and, after all, we write to read.

There is also a belief that there is only one way to spell—the right way! In fact, there is more than one way to spell a word in English and still obey the rules of English orthography. The changes in English spelling over the years and the use of variant spelling in advertising attest to this fact. Standard spelling is simply that spelling of a word which is accepted by a language community at any one time. Spelling is not static and often changes over time, although some seemingly strange spellings have been particularly resistant to change, for example, words like *through*. This leads to some variations in spelling across the English-speaking world because communities may differ, as with American and English spelling.

One of the most difficult misconceptions to counter is that language, and particularly spelling, is an absolute. This has led to some unrealistic attitudes to spelling which place impossible demands on writers, let alone young learners and their teachers. All language is contextual, and context affects the way language is used. As an aspect of language, this is no less true of spelling (Bean & Bouffler, 1987). The way we spell when we write a shopping list or take notes in a lecture is not necessarily the way we spell when we are writing a letter or proofreading an article for publication. The way we spell when we read may differ from the way we spell when we write. How often do writers confuse homophones such as *there* and *their* even when they are perfectly able to use them in their correct forms and may do so in the same text and certainly do not confuse them when they read?

We have come to accept that miscuing is part of the reading process and that all readers will miscue from time to time. Efficient readers maintain meaning when they miscue and may not even be aware that they have miscued. The more we write, the greater is the chance that we will misspell even if we are considered a good speller and, just as we may be unaware of our reading miscues, we may not see our misspellings. What we have learned about reading explains this. The more predictable the text we are reading, the less visual information we take up from the page. That which is most predictable is, of course, our own writing, especially when we have just written it, so we are less likely to see our misspellings. Thus, it is useful to distance oneself from one's writing before proofreading it.

Learning to spell

Learning to spell is a much more complex process than the traditional practice of memorising lists of words would suggest. Limitations on long- and short-term memory make deliberate memorisation difficult at best. Learning to spell involves a considerable amount of language knowledge gleaned from all aspects of language, both written and oral. This includes phonic knowledge, morphemic knowledge (how words are built up), syllabification, and semantic and syntactic knowledge.

Once they have some phonic knowledge, neophyte writers must learn English, namely, which letters go together and in what circumstances. This is the kind of knowledge that allows a writer to use a dictionary, but it is only part of the language knowledge writers need if they are to be standard spellers. They must also learn to recognise the standard form of words, to reproduce them, and to recognise deviations from the standard in texts. Learning to spell, therefore, involves learning to proofread.

To be a standard speller, we need to be able to read since it is through reading that we are given demonstrations of standard spelling. But, while reading is a necessary condition, it is not sufficient. We must also be writers. It is when we write that we discern what we need to learn from reading. While most spelling problems are first and foremost reading problems, there are those people who are considered good readers but are poor spellers. They are also reluctant writers. Spelling, especially standard spelling, is learned at the interface between reading and writing.

Children who become readers have little difficulty in becoming spellers if by spelling we mean producing spellings that obey the rules of English orthography. The problem for many children is not so much knowing how to spell but knowing what among the possible spellings of a word is the standard. This is the essential dilemma of becoming a standard speller.

There is a great deal of debate about how children become efficient written language users. While much language learning is done in natural settings under conditions of immersion, demonstration, engagement, expectation, responsibility, employment, approximation, and response as described by Cambourne (1988), there is a role for learning more explicitly about language. James Gee (1991) makes a distinction between language acquisition and language learning. I consider that Cambourne's conditions of learning describe what Gee has called *acquisition,* although I recognise these may be realised differently in different cultures. Acquisition is defined by Gee as acquiring something subconsciously. "It happens in natural settings which are meaningful and functional..." Learning, on the other hand, involves gaining conscious knowledge through teaching. "This teaching involves explanation and analysis..." [Gee (1991), cited in Mitchell & Weller, 1991, p. 5]. While I am not entirely comfortable with Gee's labelling, I find the distinction between two types of learning useful in answering the claim that whole language teachers do not explicitly teach. It is often hard to know just what is meant by *explicit teaching,* but I define it as "explanation and analysis of particular aspects of language." Therefore, where I take issue with many of our critics is not whether explicit teaching per se is appropriate, but rather what should be the content of such teaching, in what circumstances is it appropriate, and how should it be done? These questions lie at the core of all good teaching and can only be answered in terms of each individual learner.

Many whole language educators would argue that written language is acquired in ways that parallel oral language acquisition when children have opportunities to engage with print. Classrooms should create opportunities for children to acquire written language. Many critics of whole language argue that it must be learned. The reality is that language development involves both acquiring and learning. In any whole language classroom teachers set up conditions for acquiring written language while involving the learner in learning when it is necessary. Explicit teaching goes on at the point of need. It is this that distinguishes explicit teaching in a whole language classroom from explicit teaching which involves sequenced instruction and drills. Such sequences invariably follow a perceived logic which is imposed and takes little account of the complexity and often seemingly chaotic ways in which we learn what it is we know. It also makes use of text especially designed for instructional purposes rather than text written for meaning. The same critics tend to argue that teaching at the point of need is "laissez-faire." Indeed, we would argue that it is far more demanding on teachers. Not only do they have to set up conditions that will lead children to acquire the knowledge specified in state curricula outcomes, but they also need to be flexible enough to know when and how to respond to individual and class needs for more formal teaching.

Spelling in a whole language classroom

I have argued that there is no one method called whole language, nevertheless there are certain practices with regard to the teaching and learning of spelling which are likely to be found in whole language classrooms. Some of these same practices may also be found in other classrooms but are usually not integrated into a total language program.

Becoming a written language user is a developmental process. Developing as a reader and writer takes time and opportunities to engage in such practices. Becoming a standard speller also takes time and opportunities to read and write, especially to write for audiences and purposes that demand standard spelling. Whole language teachers recognise the developmental aspects of learning to spell and to proofread. In the early years of schooling, they are more likely to encourage children to write and experiment with spelling using a variety of strategies and resources to assist them. One such resource is the wall print that invariably saturates whole language classrooms.

Focussing too early on standard spelling places children in danger of becoming not only reluctant writers but of constructing themselves as poor spellers, all of which hinders writing development. Perhaps the most difficult problem for teachers in assisting children to become efficient language users is the child who will not take risks and who only writes what he or she knows how to spell in order to avoid mistakes. The role of risk taking in learning is seldom recognised by those who advocate direct, sequenced instruction. Without taking the risk that they will be wrong, learners will never push the boundaries of their learning.

Sound-symbol relationships (i.e., phonic knowledge) are important in spelling. Writing thus provides an excellent opportunity for children to acquire this knowledge. Children not learning from the demonstrations provided by print will require more explicit demonstrations. If this is necessary, the whole language teacher will teach from whole-to-part using the texts that the children are reading and writing. At all times whole language teachers strive to make language meaningful. They use meaningful situations as a basis for explanation and analysis rather than resort to the use of meaningless examples in contrived texts.

One of the difficulties in describing the teaching of spelling in whole language classrooms is that, because it is recognised as an integral part of the reading and writing processes, it is generally integrated into these practices. This means that the teaching of spelling is seldom recognised as such by the casual observer of classroom practice or by those who expect more direct approaches. Yet the reality is that whole language teachers use every opportunity to focus students on words in text as opposed to words in isolation. They use the student's own writing and a variety of written texts as sources of demonstrations about spelling. Such demonstrations focus on meaning but may include morphemic structures and patterns, some spelling rules where appropriate, and spelling paradigms. It should be noted that whole language teachers do not advocate the teaching of spelling through rules. Very few good standard spellers can articulate more than a few spelling rules. However, drawing learners' attention to particular spelling patterns, such as when to double the final consonant or drop the vowel or change the *y* to *i* before adding an additional morpheme, may be useful in assisting learners who are encountering related spelling problems.

As children develop their reading and writing they may begin to keep their own personal dictionaries with words they wish to use in their writing. These are not lists prescribed by some form of logic but lists which grow out of the children's own language use. This practice is widespread throughout the country, not just confined to whole language classrooms, although the way lists are used varies greatly. In whole language classrooms, lists are more likely to be used as ready references rather than as a source for list memorisation and testing.

Whole language teachers use a variety of teaching strategies to assist students to become proofreaders. They seek audiences for student writing, particularly audiences that demand standard spelling. They encourage students to proofread for each other. They provide support and assistance where appropriate but students are encouraged to take responsibility for proofreading their writing when it is appropriate to do so. They help their students understand the role that proofreading plays in the writing process so that they know when proofreading of one's writing is necessary and when it is not.

Summary

For critics to claim that spelling is not being taught because they have a different ideology is not just wrong, it is mischievous and unethical. My research in classrooms suggests that spelling is being taught and is often still the first thing that is addressed when students complete a piece of writing, despite the fact that this should be one of the last.

Just as there always have been, there are some students who leave school unable to use standard spelling. The high level of literacy demanded of those who are likely to succeed in this current economic rationalist world makes the problems of those young people more acute and of great concern. However, a return to past methods will not create a nation of standard spellers anymore than it did years ago and we should not pretend that it will. Similarly, we should not pretend that all students have become standard spellers in whole language classrooms. Teachers and researchers can only continue to increase their understandings and practices so that they do.

The endless debates about literacy will not solve the problems of those leaving school unable to read, write, or spell to a high standard. This is a complex social problem extending well beyond the school. Perhaps it is about time we openly recognised the political nature of literacy and the power relationships behind much of the current discourses and social practices which surround it. The way forward may well lie in changing some of these discourses and practices.

REFERENCES

Bean, W., & Bouffler, C. (1987). *Spell by writing*. Rozelle, NSW: Primary English Teaching Association.

Cambourne, B. (1988). *The whole story*. Auckland, NZ: Ashton Scholastic.

Gee, J. (1991). What is literacy? In C. Mitchell & K. Weiler (Eds.), *Rewriting literacy* (pp. 1–11). New York: Bergin & Garvey.

Yule, V. (1995). The politics of spelling. In D. Meyers (Ed.), *The multicultural imperative*. Sydney, NSW: Phadrus Books.

Real(ly) writing in school: Generic practice?

Jo-Anne Reid

In this article Jo-Anne Reid postulates the benefits of postmodern thinking in language and literacy education. She encourages literacy educators to think about what we are doing, each and every time, without relying on what we might accept (without thinking) as rules for the genre of teaching. Rather, she says, we should be engaging ourselves thoughtfully in the 'generic practice' of teaching.

All we have got are sign systems; we have no immediate access to a reality apart from a sign system. So what *licenses* any one of them? A given sign system (language, way of seeing the world, form of art, social theory, and so forth) can *claim* universality or authenticity or naturalness, but this is always a claim made from *within* the system itself. Outside the system, we are in another sign system that may well have different canons of universality or authenticity. Where do we stand to claim "authority" for ourselves and our sign systems? The postmodern answer is "nowhere." (Gee, 1993, p. 281)

A pre-position

Frances Christie's (1984) definition of genre as "any purposeful, staged, cultural activity in which human beings engage" (p. 20) was as generative for many teachers committed to whole language teaching and learning as it has been anathema to others. There is no need here to rehearse the arguments that have shot to and fro between the two schools of thought about the teaching and learning of language and literacy that have arisen since that National Reading Conference in

Perth, Australia, where Jim Martin flung the first strategic barb into an audience which rose, almost to a woman, in defence of its own. No Grave(s) digging allowed! When was that—1984, 1985? Certainly, it was a long time ago now, and we have been variously digging in, rallying round, and flying flags ever since, even though, as several commentators have demonstrated, all of this ado may really have been about nothing much at all (Comber, 1992; Kamler 1994; Kamler & Comber, 1996; Richardson, 1991). There have been many books and papers written, positions held, insults honed, and careers made over this time...and although it may not be politic to encourage such irreverent thoughts, the process-genre industry developed here in Australia during the 1980s and exported during the 1990s, has, in my opinion, been A Jolly Good Thing for all of us in the teaching profession. This is because it has caused us all to have a Jolly Good Think about what it is we do as teachers to encourage the development and expansion of language and literacy and why we do it, thereby examining the ground on which we stand to claim authority for our own particular (sign) systems for literacy education.

We've all had to take up a position—and the Jolly Postmodern has brought into our professional mail boxes many rewritings of the familiar tales about literacy learning we have taken for granted, and taken as read, as authentic and true for too long. In being forced to begin shoring up the sign system of whole language against a competing position, many in the whole language camp (who consider that we have been done wrong in this debate, and that somehow we have missed the chance to make ourselves clear and show that there was no need for all this controversy, since we had it under control all the time...) have been forced to re-examine certainties that have been challenged as inadequate and uncertain, after all. Right from the beginning, the claims of feminist and critical theorists (Gilbert, 1990; Luke, 1992), that whole language has not addressed clearly enough the hard questions of social justice and equity in education, could not be ignored—and as Christie (1990), Luke (1992), Gee (1993), and Kamler and Comber (1996) have argued, the need for a pedagogy for critical literacy in our primary schools is greatly overdue.

This is not a result of a miraculous mass hearing of continued calls for social justice, of course. It is simply an accident of history, as the world turns, inexorably, rolling onward along the conveyor belt of Fordist modernism, whirling us all, unready, into the chaotic melting pot of postmodern fast capitalism. Our uncertainty has come about because the world has changed! Things are different. We can't push the reverse button. The postmodern god-computer is now programming itself, the appalling Hansens of the world are on the move, if not in the ascendancy, and we have to learn to deal with this.

In postmodernism, "after," and "on the basis of" modernist understandings of teaching literacy, where "the system" dictates the rules of successful social textual behaviour, any certainties about what is right and proper to teach can no longer hold. Postmodernism, though, this is not a bad thing, it is only different. And we should not feel afraid or reluctant to act in such a time. Even if we can claim no authority for our sign systems and beliefs, we can examine them in relation to an ethical imperative that we must work to be sure that our actions bring no harm to others (Gee, 1993). If we continue to do this, then we will be doing something both worthwhile and, perhaps, an improvement on current practices of literacy education.

A position

In this paper, I am arguing that an emphasis on language in literacy education is no longer sufficient, and that an emphasis on the idea of social generic practice may prove to be more adequate and more helpful to learners of literacy in the postmodern era. I draw on the work of Gee (1990, 1991, 1993) and that of Green (1988, 1996) whose notion of literacy goes beyond the modernist process-genre binary. For Green (1988), a holistic view of literacy requires the acknowledgment of three related dimensions of literacy central to effective social practice: the operational, the cultural, and the critical. It is appropriate to note that this aspect of Green's work also assists us to understand and to develop approaches to information technology (IT) in schools, emphasising the need, as we rush (posthaste) towards the twenty-first century, to acknowledge the new and central position of IT in postmodern literacy education (Green, 1996).

Green's position is strongly grounded in a historical understanding of educational practice. He claims that an effective literacy curriculum for schools needs to seriously account for the critical dimensions of literacy learning, and he draws from leaders on both sides of the process-genre debate to explain the interconnection between the three dimensions of literacy. In relation to teaching he acknowledges the "first-order relationship" that exists between the *operational* and *cultural* dimensions of literacy. This, he notes, is "in accordance with the Hallidayan insight that learning language is learning culture, and vice versa." The critical dimension of literacy learning is different, however, in that it is to be understood as a second-order phenomenon, contextualising the manner in which learning how to operate in the culture involves such things as "how to best deploy its 'technologies,' and being socialised into it, becoming part of it, an 'insider'" (Green, 1996). He compares this with what has become a key referent for the whole language movement: the seven conditions for literacy learning that Cambourne (1989) has described as "a model of acquisition learning" (p. 20).

> These principles or conditions are derived from observations of "naturalistic language learning"…They attempt to take into account the nature of language learning as enculturation, i.e. the socialisation of learners into the existing socio-cultural formation, on the understanding that learning language is learning culture and vice versa. They can be seen as bringing together four kinds of learning: *enactive* learning, *iconic* learning, *verbal* learning, and *environmental* learning—put simply, learning by doing, learning by watching, learning by using verbal language (speaking, listening, writing, reading), and learning by being immersed in a certain environment over an extended period of time. The best learning situation is one which combines all of these. (Green, 1996, p. 6)

This view of critical literacy is very close to what I am calling, here, *generic practice*: the engaged production of social texts for real purposes. It is not just the provision of "good educational programmes for the teaching and learning of literacy," which Christie (1990) says "will teach explicitly the ways in which language operates" (p. 3). Indeed, it goes beyond the need to teach about literacy to encourage learning through holistic social practice. Following Gee (1990, 1991), it is clear that learning literacy involves much more than just language, and that the sort of "environmental learning" referred to above must address more than the operation of language alone. Language use always occurs in relation to symbolic, embodied, and textual practice and, in this way, the idea of generic practice links closely with Gee's explanation that any sign system in society can be understood as a "discourse." He defines discourse as

> a socially accepted association among ways of using language, of thinking, and of acting that can be used to identify oneself as a member of a socially meaningful group or "social network." (Gee, 1991, p. 1)

For Gee (1991), "Learning to read is always learning some aspect of some discourse" (p. 6). Learning to read and write successfully in school, for instance, involves much more than language. It involves learning how to hold a book, how to sit in a certain place on the mat with your body in a certain position, bringing the right sort of lunch, getting the teacher's attention, getting to know which bits of the teacher's talk you need to listen to and which bits are meant for someone else, staying awake, and the right sorts of colours to use for colouring with your crayons (Kamler, Maclean, Reid, & Simpson, 1995). Learning a discourse can be thought of as acquiring "an 'identity kit' which comes complete with the appropriate costume and instructions on how to act and talk so as to take on a particular role that others will recognize" (Gee, 1991, p. 1).

A proposition

Learning to write and speak about things that matter, in recognisable ways that will get you read and heard in social life, requires the textual crafting of your meaning to become transparent, invisible. The meaning *is* the message. As you read this paper, it has been my intention thus far to slightly jar and fracture the lines and planes of the textual form so as to make the nature of the text itself the object of your attention from time to time—not "as well as my meaning," for this is, of course, my meaning. My alliterations and allusions are a sort of textual display, that, for this type of article, seems somehow, generically immodest. However I'm not actually worried by this transgression, only somewhat concerned that the Jolly Postman joke was too obscure and no one but me will even groan at its ham-fistedness.

Besides which, this text is *not* massively transgressive, is it? You may, quite honestly, not even have noticed. The medium has become the message, harking (effectively) back to the artistic, cubist, McLuhanistic, even as it moves forward to the postmodern. And it still feels like an educational argument. Although, please note that I have not allowed the sorts of cracks into the surface of my text that could appear as defects in my capacity to craft a good, solid text —I make sure my spelling is correct, for instance, and my commas are carefully controlled. I am not indiscreet: I do not wish to be thought a novice, a learner-writer.

Like any genre, the journal article can be thought of as a purposeful, staged, cultural activity. The conventions can be (and are) explicitly taught to academic writers around the nation. Yet knowing the rules of the journal article genre will not necessarily get me published. What matters, more than knowing and being able to utilise the conventional way to say what I have to say, is knowing how to fashion it in a way that will be heard as I want it to. This is not a new argument, of course, but it is not one that is clearly enough heard by teachers—especially when the outcomes statements to which we are oriented describe our teaching-learning goals in such very conventional frameworks. In the terms I am using here, we can help our students learn operational and cultural literacies through attention to the process and genres of textual production in classrooms, but we often fall short of providing them with access to critical literacies—which are most meaningfully produced in and through fully realised, social, textual practice.

To provide a critical distance from my own generic practice in this text, I will go on in the next section to provide critical instance of a common purposeful, staged, cultural activity, engaged with as generic practice in everyday life. I will first demonstrate how the appearance of rule-governance is just a mirage, but that strategic tactical decisions need to be made as part of larger generic practices specific to particular situations of practice. In postmodern terms, I don't need to know or understand information to use it (Green, 1995). I shall illustrate how textual practice parallels this generic practice in several important ways. And, I will conclude by rehearsing ways in which textual practice can become generic practice in the primary classroom by means of renewed attention to literacy practices that re-emphasise reasons for writing (and reading), including those associated with pleasure, play, and pastiche.

A meaty argument

Imagine, for a moment, you are not a vegetarian. For most (mainstream) Australian people this will come very easily. For others it will require a cultural and perhaps spiritual and emotional upheaval, resulting in uncertainty, unease, and perhaps even unhappiness. But, as readers of my text you have only a limited range of possible options for action at this moment. You can, perhaps, quite comfortably, go along with my request because you do not find it unreasonable or unsettling. You might feel compromised by my use of authorial power to control your actions. But yet, you may still do as I ask—because you are a good subject of the text and trust that in going along with me you may experience or learn something that will, though difficult and even unnatural for you, ultimately be of some benefit. Or you can resist this suggestion as being insensitive, carnivorous, and against all your beliefs and inclinations. You might, then, decide to simply sit back and observe, perhaps just going through the motions till the next heading. Or, knowing that you could never want not to be a vegetarian, you might decide this is not for you.

So, then, supposing you are not a vegetarian, you need to get meat to eat. Like literacy, food is a basic. All non-vegetarians need to get their meat from somewhere. Buying the meat, I suggest, is an important genre in our culture. It can quite easily be seen as a purposeful, staged, cultural activity, like a fairy tale or a written argument. Yet instantly, as soon as we reflect on the stages that mark the achievement of this very practical goal, we can see that the meat purchasing genre, like all genres, is extremely complex, and in effect is a diversified accumulation of different sign systems in practice. It is very clear, for example, that today, depending on where you live, your needs, resources, constraints, and the nature of the local society, the social practice of buying your meat can be very different generically and could be almost impossible to actually teach to someone as a set of rules.

To start with, there are still people in our society who don't buy the meat they eat, needing or choosing to butcher their own. Fifty years ago just about all of us who did not fall into that group bought (or bartered) meat from a butcher. Today, for instance, in urban areas, we have the choice to buy our meat from a butcher's shop or from the supermarket. And while the vast majority of us still buy meat that has been killed and cut by a butcher, in our postmodern world it is possible that we may never see, interact with, or even know who or where that butcher is (let alone where he has been).

The surfaces of the social texts of our meat buying can therefore be very different, even though we will all achieve the same outcomes. We do this by following only one generic rule: Get your meat. In postmodern late capitalism, there can also be goal variations on this genre, of course: Get your meat as cheaply as possible; get the best value in meat available; get the choicest cut of meat you can; get your meat kosher; get your meat delivered; get three rashers of rindless bacon; which will all, in themselves, determine the strategies you employ as you engage in the generic practice of meat getting.

How will you enter the shop? Will you have to brush through the plastic fly strips, stand in front of the automatic door-opening sensor, walk past the ice cream shop to the mall display counter, push your trolley to aisle 17, or pick up the telephone? Will you speak to anyone? Yes, no, perhaps. Who will you speak to? The butcher, the apprentice butcher, the sales person, the woman offering samples from the lamb marketing board, the lady behind you in line, the check-out operator, nobody at all. I won't go on. You recognise all these variations. You can make your own potential generic practice with regard to questions such as:

- When will you speak?

- What will you say?

- How will you say it?

- How will you select your meat?

- How will you get it?

• How will you pay for it?

The important points are these. You don't and can't know what decisions you will actually have to make until you are actually engaged in the generic practice of your particular situation. Even then, you will find that you need to adapt the rules you may have been told about how to buy meat or have discerned for yourself through observation and shared experience. It is quite clear that these are not rules which govern the situation at all. They are practical options which frame it for you, and they are available to you in the practice of the genre through generic practice. Once you are sufficiently practised, they allow you to buy your meat without so much as a second thought, for much of the time. But whenever something unexpected happens or something in the situation changes, you will once again become conscious of them. And there will be no rules to guide you when this happens. You will act according to your most pressing needs at the time. Imagine, for instance, the effect on your will, budget, and shopping list, of the spontaneous vision of the effect, on your new non-vegetarian lover, of sharing that succulent rack of spring lamb you've suddenly noticed to the left of the Chicken Kiev. It's the first of the season, it would be surrounded by new potatoes and long green beans, dripping with red-wine gravy and mint sauce. Forget what your friends say about it being absolutely essential to have everything pre-prepared for the first meal together, with nothing troublesome (like gravy) to distract your pre-dinner drinks. The lamb, you think, may just be a jolly good thing—regardless of the rules—a strategy that might work to achieve your purpose!

A re-position

Taking us back to basics here, then, is the question begged in this example, particularly in the paragraph above. What happens when you are not well practised at all; when you are just practising, learning what it means to engage in the generic practice of meat buying, producing a journal article, constructing a narrative, or even recounting what you did at the Royal Show last week.

To answer this, let us reconsider for a moment how we learned to buy meat. For some of us, this was extremely easy. We learnt "for free," as Gee (1991) would say—perhaps, quite literally, at our mother's knee—as we were first carried, then pushed in our strollers, and then finally obliged to follow her in pre-school shoes through the rounds of the shopping, looking up quietly, waiting, but knowing not to ask, for the hoped for (but always only half-expected) piece of polony or frankfurt. We learnt the smell and the sawdust. We know about butchers' paper, the wooden chopping block, and the clink of the butcher's knives as he drew them from his belt to sharpen against the steel hanging by a thin rope from a hook on the wall. Since then, we haven't consciously noted the changes to the generic practice of meat buying. But when the smells changed, when the sawdust disappeared, and the plastic fern appeared in the window, our practice also changed. We accepted the convenience of the supermarket meat counter perhaps, though always keeping up the appearances of good relations with our local butcher, just in case. And we can tell a good cut of meat, and we know the difference between a good sausage and a poor one. And further, we also know (Cambourne, 1988; Gee, 1991, 1993; Heath, 1983; Luke, 1992) that some children in our schools learn to read and write in exactly the same way as they learn to buy meat. Easily, naturally, almost without thinking.

For others though, this is not the way your people get meat, or you become literate. Some people's fathers meet at the co-op once a week and take their share from the communal purchase. Others drive to the cold storage once every two months and purchase a freezer load in bulk. Other people buy meat fresh every day. These might be, or might not be, among those who choose meat from plastic-covered packets displayed on supermarket shelves. The variety of generic practices is large, though it is not infinite. Nor is it infinitely varied. If you have never had the opportunity to watch someone else select and size up a veal rump before the butcher slices it, you may not have the power to go to him to ask for it to be cut, just so. Instead you will pick up a package of thin sliced Vienna schnitzel pre-cut from the display cabinet. The point is, there is not just one way to achieve your ends. If you want meat, even if you don't have the means to obtain it, you will strategically adapt and accommodate your actions to the generic practice of getting it—in practice, as you go. And to do this you will draw on the range of practices available to you to achieve this end, even if they are not exactly kosher. To learn to buy meat well involves much more than just the purposeful stages of selecting, asking, and paying. It may also involve talking to strangers; deferring to powerful men; writing lists; enlisting the help of a friend; reading magazines, cookbooks, and novels; watching television; going to restaurants; imagining tastes; estimating weights; and the multiplication, addition, and subtraction of numbers.

It is the same with writing. There is always more involved in the production of a text than can be ordered or governed. We learn generic literacies in practice. We will only learn to write good letters by wanting or needing to write them, but learning to write letters may also involve taking messages, telling anecdotes, talking on the telephone, reading books, watching television and movies, copying down addresses onto envelopes, and reading letters ourselves. We learn to make arguments by wanting things; feeling unfairly treated; and observing the way other people convince, move, or influence us and others (or fail to do these things).

We get better at doing these things by practising them, of course, until we too can do many of the things involved in making an argument, writing a narrative, or constructing a dialogue, without thinking about it unless something unexpected occurs. We learn to tell stories by stretching our imagination, rearranging ideas from our lives, reading, watching or listening to television, attending movies, using the Internet and computer games, forming our own fantasies, and listening to other people's gossip. In this way, the literacies we value in schools can be understood as generic. They are, in practice, "general, not specific or special" (*Australian Oxford Dictionary*). And yet most of the time in schools we value or reward only a narrow range of conventionally powerful strategies for achieving a particular outcome. Other ways are seen as wrong, inadequate, or unconventional. When this happens, it is clear, as Gee (1993) writes:

> Schools can only expect opposition from those children and their families whom they either exclude or seek to apprentice to practices that are

owned and operated by groups who otherwise oppose and oppress them in the wider society outside the school. (p. 291)

Critical literacy practice in schools, then, must be generic practice, where children can tactically select from all the operational strategies available in the cultures available to them, rather than being taught one, conventionally most strategic operation. Through generic practice, learners can experience which of their generic tactics pay off and which don't work for particular purposes or on particular audiences. They can sit back and watch the practical effects of their literacy on others. And, they won't just have one set of powerful rules to draw from.

We can no longer rely on such a modernist logic to guide us through the teaching of literacy now that we realise that the learning of literacy does not work like that. In postmodern literacy education, we learn (and teach) powerful literacies through powerful literacy practices, not just through the operational and cultural dimensions of literacy learning. In *The Practice of Everyday Life*, Michel de Certeau (1984) introduced a world teetering on the end of the modernist production line to the concept of the "tactic," a practical answer for dealing with the structures (and strategies) of powerful sign systems and institutions in ways that are useful and effective at the time, to suit the constantly changing and unpredictable needs of the user, as well as the system.

De Certeau (1984) sees these strategies as transitory, fragmentary, "insinuating" themselves into the place of the conventional, orderly, and rule-governed behaviour "without taking it over" but also "without being able to keep it at a distance":

> [B]ecause it does not have a place, a tactic depends on time—it is always on the watch for opportunities that must be seized "on the wing." Whatever it wins it does not keep. It must constantly manipulate events in order to turn them into "opportunities." (p. xix)

The tactics used by a writer, speaker, or buyer of meat to get what she wants—this time, here, now—are developed in and from the generic practice itself. For de Certeau (1984) they are "achieved in the propitious moments when they are able to combine heterogeneous elements" (p. xix) of a situation, in practice. The child learning to write must be encouraged to write in ways which reward her attempts to sample, copy, borrow, quote, and utilise everything within all available sign systems, to get the job done. There is not just one right way. Not any longer. Operational and cultural literacies are "strategies" in de Certeau's terms. Critical literacy is derived from tactical attempts to use literacy to get things done. In practice, "the intellectual synthesis of [the] given elements takes the form [...] of the decision itself, the act and manner in which the opportunity is 'seized'" (de Certeau, 1984, p. xix). Learners of literacy need to experience and reflect on the effects of their practice on other people. They need to talk about the effects of other people's practice on themselves. Without this they cannot learn to question the undoubtable truth of reading material nor to doubt the unquestionable logic of any one best way.

A postposition

As Gee (1993) writes: "Education is always and everywhere the initiation of students as apprentices into various historically situated social practices so that they become 'insiders'" (p. 291). But then he goes on, immediately, reminding us that nothing, any longer, is certain: "Or," he says, "it is the exclusion of children from these apprenticeships."

Simple reminders like this clearly underline the benefits of postmodern thinking. It is a Jolly Good Thing to have doubt. Doubt encourages us to have a Jolly Good Think about what we are doing each and every time, without relying on what we might accept (without thinking) as rules for the genre of teaching—rather than engaging ourselves thoughtfully in the generic practice of teaching.

REFERENCES

Cambourne, B. (1989). Look what they've done to my song, ma: A reply to Luke, Baty & Stehbens. *English in Australia, 90,* 13–22.

Christie, F. (1984). Varieties of written discourse. In F. Christie & Course Team (Eds.), *Children writing: Study guide* (pp. 11–52). Geelong, Victoria: Deakin University Press.

Christie, F. (1990). The changing face of literacy. In F. Christie (Ed.), *Literacy for a changing world* (pp. 1–25). Hawthorn, Victoria: Australian Council of Education Research.

Comber, B. (1992). Critical literacy: A selective review and discussion of recent literature. *South Australian Educational Leader, 3*(1), 1–10.

de Certeau, M. (1984). *The practice of everyday life* (S.F. Rendell, Trans.). Berkeley, CA: University of California Press.

Gee, J.P. (1990). *Social linguistics and literacies. Ideology in discourses*. Basingstoke, UK: Falmer Press.

Gee, J.P. (1991). What is literacy? In C. Mitchell & K. Weiler (Eds.), *Rewriting literacy* (pp. 1–11). New York: Bergin & Garvey.

Gee, J.P. (1993). Postmodernism and literacies. In C. Lankshear & P.L. McLaren (Eds.), *Critical literacy: Politics, praxis, and the postmodern* (pp. 271–295). Albany, NY: State University of New York Press.

Gilbert, P. (1990). Authorizing disadvantage: Authorship and creativity in the language classroom. In F. Christie (Ed.), *Literacy for a changing world* (pp. 54–78). Melbourne, Victoria: Australian Council of Education Research.

Green, B. (1988). Subject-specific literacy and school learning: A focus on writing. *Australian Journal of Education, 32*(2), 156–179.

Green, B. (1995). *On compos(IT)ing: Writing differently in the post-age*. Paper presented at the Australian Association for the Teaching of English National Conference, Sydney, NSW.

Green, B. (1996). *Literacy/technology/learning: Notes and issues*. Discussion Paper DEET Project: The Role and Status of Technology in Language and Literacy Learning. Geelong, Victoria: Deakin Centre for Education and Change.

Heath, S.B. (1983). *Ways with words*. Cambridge, UK: Cambridge University Press.

Kamler, B. (1994). Resisting oppositions in writing pedagogy, or what process-genre debate? *Idiom, 29*(2), 14–19.

Kamler, B., Maclean, R., Reid, J., & Simpson, A. (1995). *Shaping up nicely: The formation of schoolgirls and schoolboys in the first month of school*. Canberra, Western Capital Territory: Department of Employment, Education and Training.

Kamler, B., & Comber, B. (1996). Critical literacy: Not generic–not developmental–not another orthodoxy. *Changing Education, 3*(1), 1–6.

Luke, A. (1992). The social construction of literacy in the primary school. In L. Unsworth (Ed.), *Literacy learning and teaching: Language as social practice in the primary school* (pp. 1–53). Melbourne, Victoria: Macmillan.

Richardson, P. (1991). Language as personal resource and as social construct: Competing views of literacy pedagogy in Australia. *Educational Review, 43*(2), 171–189.

Whole language and its critics: A New Zealand perspective

John Smith

Adversaries of whole language claim that it is a "passing fad" without a valid research base. What motivates such claims? Is there any substance to them? In his article, Smith examines the validity of the attack and presents some research-based counter-arguments.

Attacks on whole language

Whole language teachers often find themselves under attack from two quarters: Some politicians who, allied with the daily press, often find an attack on "declining literacy standards" provides publicity and the appearance of doing something about a complex problem; and some university researchers who claim that there is no evidence to support whole language.

Typically, these attacks are politically motivated. A trend throughout the Western world for the last decade has been for government to reduce spending by divesting itself of many of its businesses. Thus state-owned airlines, telephone systems, and banks have been privatised; welfare payments have been either frozen or cut; and education spending has been static. Conservative governments, whether in New Zealand, Australia, Great Britain, or the United States, have fostered a view that all government activity, including education, is inherently suspect and a much greater accountability is required.

While I have no difficulty with accountability in education, I have extreme difficulty with an accountability system that reduces complex problems to over-simple boxes to be ticked. Political demands, couched in the form of simplistic performance standards, may force a technicist-view of reading into classrooms.

Media criticisms

A recent report in a New Zealand newspaper described schools in New York thus:

> The latest term began with 90,000 more pupils than places and reports of lessons in corridors and changing rooms and children forced to sit on the floor because there were not enough chairs. Some schools are even working in shifts. As well the threat of drugs and violence hangs over many schools in the poorer districts, where children enter through metal detectors and leave barely able to read and write. (*Sunday Star-Times*, December 15, 1996, p. C6)

Against this depressing picture, politicians seize on simplistic explanations and apportion blame in the way that serves them best in the polls. They claim that the causes of under-achievement in our schools are not due to the social conditions many children are forced to live in, or to underfunded schools, or underpaid teachers, but to "progressive methods" or to "whole language" teaching. A companion article to the one cited above claims:

> The decline in standards (in U.S. schools) has been traced by some critics to a teaching fad called "whole language." (*Sunday Star-Times*, December 15, 1996, p. C6).

Similarly, New Zealand critics attribute any difficulties children have with literacy to teaching methods. During the past year we too have had newspaper and television reports about New Zealand children beginning high school who are unable to read.

Standardised test scores are typically offered as evidence of decline, but most experts agree that standardised tests sample a very limited range of reading behaviours and lack external validity. How often are we asked to read something and then answer ten multi-choice questions about it? Standardised tests cannot reveal whether children read voluntarily, how well they select and skim, or whether they enjoy reading. Nor do they take into account the social and cultural differences between children. Furthermore, the data from the International Association for the Evaluation of Educational Achievement (IEA) surveys do not support claims that "whole language has failed." The 1990 IEA survey showed that New Zealand children were the highest achievers of the English-speaking nations, and fourth overall (Elley, 1992). The question which required students to report how they became good readers was answered by the top 20 percent of readers in each country. They claimed that good reading required "having lots of good books around" and "using your imagination." By contrast, the best readers in the countries where failure rates were highest believed it was important to "sound out the words correctly" and "to have lots of practice at the hard things" (Elley, 1992).

An analysis of the top and bottom twenty schools in the New Zealand IEA sample (when the influence of home background was controlled) showed that high-achieving schools had all implemented whole language principles (Elley, 1992). All had enthusiastic reading teachers on staff, all were well-stocked with quality books, and regular homework was the rule. A distinctive feature of the low-achieving schools was a greater emphasis on decontextualised phonics teaching (Elley, 1992). Such evidence contradicts superficial media criticisms of whole language teaching.

Academic criticisms of whole language

Academic critics face a dilemma in their work. In order to gain publication in refereed international journals, they need to meet the research criteria laid down by the academic disciplines within whose frameworks they operate. In the prevailing paradigm this means they need to standardise their experimental procedures. This in turn means they must use contrived, decontextualised, artificial, one-shot methods to measure reading ability. Whole language researchers reject such methods, preferring to use methods from a different scientific paradigm. This is one which allows for data to be collected from a variety of texts and contexts, which uses multiple cues to meaning, and involves prolonged periods of careful and rigorous observation. While elegantly designed experimental studies with complex statistical analyses may be interesting to read, their findings are of limited value because they lack ecological validity. The enormous gap between the contrived nature of such research and the daily ebb and flow of classrooms is simply too great to validate the results of such research.

Technicist criticisms of whole language

Learning to read is not a natural act like learning to speak. Rather, it requires specific tuition, and recognition that sounds are represented by letters.

It is true that some children have great difficulty learning to read, whereas all children do learn to speak. However, there are data which show that if children are immersed in high-interest print, given real purposes for learning to read it, and are in the company of people who can read and are interested in reading, they will acquire by themselves the understanding that sounds are represented by letters and learn these letter-sound links along with the other cues for meaning (Elley, 1991, 1992). How else can we explain how children learn to read at home without formal tuition (Clark, 1976; Durkin, 1976)? Furthermore, while specific tuition about letters and sounds may help some children when they read, it may also convey the wrong impressions about the difficulty and purposes of reading (Rousch & Cambourne, 1979). We know too that it is possible for readers to go directly from print to meaning without lessons on sounding out (Crystal, 1994; Rayner & Pollatsek, 1989). Thousands of semantically acceptable miscues confirm this point (Rousch & Cambourne, 1979). When children read *sleeping* for *asleep* and *said Mum* for *Mother said*, they are clearly going straight from print to meaning and then formulating the sound. Perhaps time spent on developing emergent readers' ability to sound may be counterproductive for later silent reading? As Smith once noted, "Phonics is easy, if you already have a good idea of what the word is in the first place" (Smith, 1983, p. 31).

Prediction is not an efficient strategy to teach children. Studies show that words in English are not predictable and that good readers don't predict.

This is a red herring because it assumes that effective reading depends on errorless reproduction of what's on the page. Miscue research shows clearly that effective readers do not predict isolated words, they predict meanings (Rousch & Cambourne, 1979). This is a very different process from predicting words.

Eye movement research shows that skilled readers actually fixate on almost every word of text. They do not predict, sample, and confirm as many whole language theorists claim.

This evidence is not conclusive. Just because the eyes fixate on something does not mean that the brain sees or attends to it. It's scientifically irresponsible to suggest otherwise. We cannot see into readers' minds to determine whether every word and every letter is examined or whether just the beginnings and ends of words are examined. We also do not know whether reading a book chosen by the child and perused in the book corner differs from reading text where the reader's eye movements are being photographed in laboratory.

Research studies show that phonological awareness increases children's test scores and should be taught systematically.

Phonological awareness is taught in whole language classrooms (Cambourne, 1997). Every time children read a shared book about Leo the Lion, and the teacher or a child comments that *Leo* and *Lion* begin with the same letters that have the same sound, phonological awareness is being taught. However it is taught within the context of a meaningful story and is one facet of reading, secondary to understanding and enjoyment. Discussion of words, letters, and sounds is a part of whole language classrooms, but it arises from and supports the meaning and enjoyment of the story.

Summaries of comparative studies conducted for the most part in the United States tend to show that "code-oriented" emphases produce better results than meaning-orientated methods (Chall, 1983; Adams, 1990).

Such reviews need to be interpreted with caution, and some researchers reject them outright for using irrelevant criteria to make invalid comparisons (Carbo, 1988). It is important to note that contrast programs used in the United States rarely have the kinds of components found in New Zealand whole language programs. It is also true that many are evaluated on very restricted criteria, such as word recognition or tests of phonological skills or artificial exercises. American standardised tests, in the early grades, stress decoding skills. Whole language aims for a much broader range of outcomes. Nevertheless, the claim that hard evidence is lacking on the benefits of whole language methods, such as those used in New Zealand, can be rejected in the light of the following empirical studies.

1. New Zealand children who typically learn by whole language methods consistently achieve at very high levels in international studies of reading and literature interpretation (Elley, 1992; Purves, 1973; Thorndike, 1973).

2. Singapore children also scored at high levels in the recent IEA study despite their relatively low levels of economic and social development, and despite the fact that they learned to write in a non-native language (Elley, 1992). The distinctive feature of their early programs is that they too learn by language experience, shared reading, and immersion in high-interest print. When comparisons were conducted in Singapore of this style of program and more structured phonic programs, the former proved consistently better (Elley, 1991).

3. A series of empirical studies conducted in the United States by Lesley Morrow (1989, 1990, 1992) has shown extensive benefits for many of the features of whole language programs. For instance, in one study (Morrow, 1992) the progress of nine Grade 2 classes in the Unites States was studied in a literature-based program which provided a rich literacy environment and regular story reading by teachers, with discussion and lots of self-directed reading and writing. The theoretical rationale drew on the work of Holdaway (1979), Cambourne (1988), and Teale (1984), all proponents of whole language approaches. Morrow found substantial increases, relative to control groups, in story comprehension, oral retellings, written retellings, oral and written creation of stories, diversity of vocabulary use, and complexity of sentences. The literature-based program also provided more positive attitudes in pupils and led to more voluntary book reading.

4. Many of the component features of the whole language programs have been evaluated separately using standardised tests and have been found to produce strong results. The following are examples.

Shared reading. This method, when used with high-interest reading materials, proved very effective in promoting reading comprehension, word recognition, and oral language in a Vuie study (Elley, 1980;

De'Ath, 1980) and in promoting reading, writing, listening, vocabulary, and grammar in the Fiji book flood study (Elley & Mangubhai, 1983). It also produced positive attitudes and better reading test scores in a New Zealand survey (Elley, 1985).

Silent reading. Empirical studies of the benefits of silent reading for improving achievement in reading are increasing—for examples, see Anderson, Wilson, and Fielding (1988); Stanovich (1992); Taylor, Pyro, and Marvgumma (1990); and Krashen (1988). The IEA survey (1992) showed that countries which allocate more time to silent reading produced better test results, other things being equal. Also, recent studies of the extent of exposure to print show promising correlations with achievement (Stanovich, 1992). The Fiji book flood study (Elley & Mangubhai, 1983) and several other studies of regular exposure to books produced similarly encouraging findings about the important benefits of regular silent reading.

Story reading aloud. Whole language supporters usually emphasise the important role of story reading to children. Holdaway (1979) has spelled out a number of benefits; Durkin (1976) and Clark (1976) show that early readers are much read to at home; Wells (1986) showed substantial benefits of story reading in his longitudinal studies.

Summary

It is impossible to answer all the criticisms of whole language. However, criticisms from the media and politicians (usually comprising unsourced anecdotes) and those from university researchers (which emerge from the confines of a narrow technicist view of reading) can and should be answered. Remember: For every complex problem, there is a simple solution—which is always wrong.

REFERENCES

Adams, M. (1990). *Beginning to read.* Cambridge, MA: Massachusetts Insitute of Technology Press.

Anderson, R., Wilson P., & Fielding, J. (1988). Growth in reading and how children spend their time out of school. *Reading Research Quarterly, 53,* 285–303.

Cambourne, B. (1988). *The whole story: Natural learning and the acquisition of literacy in the classroom.* Auckland, NZ: Ashton Scholastic.

Cambourne, B. (1997). Ideology and the teaching of phonics: An Australian perspective. In A. Marek & C. Edelsky (Eds.), *A Festschrift for Kenneth Goodman.* New York, NY: Macmillan.

Carbo, M. (1988, November). Debunking the great phonics myth. *Phi Delta Kappan*, 226–240.

Chall, J. (1983). *Stages of reading development.* New York: McGraw-Hill.

Clark, M. (1976). *Young fluent readers.* London: Heinemann.

De'Ath, P. (1980). The shared book experience and ESL. *Directions, 4,* 13–22.

Durkin, D. (1976). A six-year study of children who learned to read in school at the age of four. *Reading Research Quarterly, 10,* 9–61.

Elley, W. (1980). A comparison on content-interest and structuralist reading programmes in Nule primary schools. *New Zealand Journal of Educational Studies, 15*(1).

Elley, W. (1991). Acquiring literacy in a second language: The effect of book-based programmes. *Language Learning, 41,* 375–411.

Elley, W. (1992). *How in the world do students read?* The Hague, Netherlands: International Association for the Evaluation of Education Achievement.

Elley, W. (1985). *Lessons learned about LARIC.* Christchurch, NZ: University of Canterbury Education Department.

Elley, W., & Mangubhai, F. (1983). The impact of reading on second language learning. *Reading Research Quarterly, 9,* 53–67.

Holdaway, D. (1979). *The foundations of literacy.* Gosford, NSW: Ashton Scholastic.

Krashen, S. (1988). Do we learn to read by reading? The relationship between free reading and reading ability. In D. Tannen (Ed.), *Linguistics in context.* Norwood, NJ: Ablex.

Morrow, L. (1992). The impact of a literature-based programme on literacy achievement, use of literature and attitudes of children from minority background. *Reading Research Quarterly, 27,* 250–275.

Purves, A. (1973). *Literature education in ten countries.* Stockholm, Sweden: Almquist & Wiksell.

Rayner, K., & Pollatsek, A. (1989). *The psychology of reading.* (ERIC Document Reproduction Service No. ER 301851).

Smith, F. (1983). *Essays into literacy.* Portsmouth, NH: Heinemann.

Stanovich, K. (1992). The psychology of reading: Evolutionary and revolutionary developments. *Annual Review of Applied Linguistics, 12,* 3–30.

Taylor, B., Pyro, B., & Marvgumma, M. (1990). Time spent reading and reading growth. *American Educational Research Journal, 27,* 351–362.

Teale, W. (1984). Reading to young children: Its significance for literacy development. In A. Oberg & F. Smith (Eds.), *Awakening to literacy.* London, UK: Heinemann.

Wells, G. (1986). *The meaning makers: Children learning language and using language to learn.* Portsmouth, NH: Heinemann.

DATE DUE